PRAISE FOR
THE QUOTABLE ROGUE

If you learned everything you knew about American politics from Matt Lewis, you'd be in pretty good shape. I should know, since I practically do.

TUCKER CARLSON, COFOUNDER AND EDITOR-IN-CHIEF OF *THE DAILY CALLER*

Matt Lewis is a conservative provocateur and has an easy way of making complicated issues understandable and leaving the D. C. jargon off the table. Matt's projects always make you think, reflect, and act.

GOVERNOR RICK PERRY, 47TH GOVERNOR OF TEXAS

Sarah Palin is one of the most important conservative leaders in America—and Matt Lewis is one of my favorite writers. Every conservative ought to have a copy of the *Quotable Rogue* in their personal library—if for no other reason than to refute the distortions and lies constantly hurled at Palin by her detractors.

KEN BLACKWELL, FORMER OHIO SECRETARY OF STATE, SENIOR FELLOW AT THE FAMILY RESEARCH COUNCIL

For all the accolades heaped on Mr. Obama for his soaring rhetoric and brilliant, professorial oratory, it's hard to deny that Sarah Palin is one of the most quotable leaders of the 21st century. *The Quotable Rogue* brings that into stunning clarity. And it's not because she's controversial—it's because she's usually just right.

S.E. CUPP, POLITICAL COLUMNIST AND CULTURE CRITIC, AUTHOR OF *LOSING OUR RELIGION: THE LIBERAL MEDIA'S ATTACK ON CHRISTIANITY*

As you'll see in Matt's book, the reason for Sarah Palin's popularity is that she speaks in a blunt fashion and exposes truths that the politically correct job-protecting elites are fearful of. She is a far wiser woman than Katie Couric.

ANDREW BREITBART, BREITBART.COM, AUTHOR OF *RIGHTEOUS INDIGNATION*

Sarah Palin drives the left crazy and makes many of the Republicans who collaborated with Democrats to destroy our fiscal wellbeing duck and cover. Matt Lewis captures, through Sarah Palin's own words, her wit, wisdom, and basic sense that America remains the last best hope for mankind.

ERICK ERICKSON, EDITOR-IN-CHIEF OF REDSTATE.COM

Steadfast in her beliefs and fearless in her demeanor, Sarah Palin has become a leading voice in today's conservative movement and has inspired a new generation of activists. This book of quotes captures the independent spirit of Palin and is a great resource for all of us who are 'going rogue' alongside her.

TERI CHRISTOPH, COFOUNDER, SMART GIRL POLITICS

A book like this one is absolutely essential in a world where the media refuses to quote Gov. Palin without liberal doses of snark, vitriol, and hyperbole. It's refreshing to see straight quotes in print so that readers can make up their own minds.

ADAM BRICKLEY, FOUNDER, "DRAFT SARAH PALIN FOR VICE PRESIDENT"

THE
QUOTABLE
ROGUE

THE

QUOTABLE ROGUE

The Ideals of
SARAH PALIN
in Her Own Words

Edited by Matt Lewis

THOMAS NELSON
Since 1798

NASHVILLE   DALLAS   MEXICO CITY   RIO DE JANEIRO

Published in Nashville, Tennessee, by Thomas Nelson. Thomas Nelson is a registered trademark of Thomas Nelson, Inc.

Thomas Nelson, Inc., titles may be purchased in bulk for educational, business, fund-raising, or sales promotional use. For information, please e-mail SpecialMarkets@ThomasNelson.com.

Library of Congress Cataloging-in-Publication Data

The quotable rogue : the ideals of Sarah Palin in her own words / edited by Matt Lewis.
    p. cm.
  ISBN 978-1-59555-356-0
  1. United States—Politics and government—2009—Quotations, maxims, etc.
  2. Palin, Sarah, 1964—Quotations. 3. Palin, Sarah, 1964—Political and social views. I. Palin, Sarah, 1964– II. Lewis, Matt.
  F910.7.P35A25 2011
  081—dc22
                        2011010631

Printed in the United States of America

11 12 13 14 15 RRD 6 5 4 3 2 1

CONTENTS

FOREWORD

Before most Americans knew the name Sarah Palin, I blogged about this exciting conservative governor from Wasilla, Alaska. And in July of 2008, virtually on the eve of her selection as John McCain's running mate, I authored a post titled "The Conservative Guide to VP Picks." I argued that McCain should consider Palin because, as I reasoned, "she would excite conservatives."

She did!

The Palin pick immediately motivated conservatives *and* boosted John McCain's poll numbers. For a brief time after picking Sarah Palin as his running mate, McCain actually led in the polls. In August of 2008, immediately after Palin's announcement, I blogged that "the mood around the offices of Townhall.com [a conservative blog where I was then employed] is sort of like that of Christmastime."

As a credentialed blogger at the 2008 Republican National Convention in Minneapolis, Minnesota, I was fortunate to be inside the packed auditorium when Sarah Palin gave her electrifying convention speech. One can only imagine what the mood of the convention would have been like had McCain picked moderate Republican (and former Pennsylvania governor) Tom Ridge—or Democrat Joe Lieberman (as he reportedly *wanted* to do). My guess is the convention would have been a disaster, but McCain's selection of Palin gave his campaign a much-needed boost that August.

While I had been an admirer of Palin's fiscal conservatism in Alaska, the role she adopted during the campaign, coupled with the "lamestream" media's portrayal of Palin, painted her as primarily a social conservative. Palin's pre-veep identity was as a leading reformer and fiscal conservative . . . a starkly different image from what most Americans now know.

It's also true that many "Palinisms" have been invented by the media, or, to paraphrase Yogi Berra: "She never said most of the things she said." For example, we all remember Tina Fey's line, "I can see Russia from my house!" But as my former editor, Carl Cannon, pointed out in a *Politics Daily* column, what Palin actually said was, "They're our next door neighbors, and you can actually see Russia from land here in Alaska, from an island in Alaska." That, of course, is not nearly as funny (or silly).

Who knows what the future will hold for Sarah Palin, but whatever you think of her, she is clearly a powerful force in politics and in the culture.

Matt Lewis

INTRODUCTION

From the moment she took the stage at an Ohio campaign rally on August 29, 2008, Sarah Palin became a dynamic part of America's political and cultural landscape. When Republican presidential candidate John McCain stepped to the podium and introduced the then-Alaska governor as his vice-presidential running mate, few Americans had even heard of her. Fewer still knew who she was or where she stood on the key issues of the day.

Not for long. In the hours and days that followed, the media beamed a spotlight on Palin: her family of five children (including an infant son with Down syndrome) and her snow machine-racing husband; her thin political pedigree, featuring stints as a school board member and small-town mayor before she rose to the governorship; and her rural upbringing in the wilds of Alaska, where she often accompanied her father on predawn moose hunts.

Palin's journey from obscurity to celebrity was as rapid as it was unlikely. She seemed so ordinary. And yet she quickly became a household name, a recognizable face, and a lightning rod for strong reactions.

As anyone who was paying attention during the fall of 2008 knows, Palin tended to embody polarization during the campaign, inspiring equal parts adoration and vitriol. She was beloved by conservatives, disdained by liberals, carefully studied by centrist independents, and dissected relentlessly by an insatiable media machine.

Would it be fair to say that perceptions of her depended largely on the perceiver? As Palin might put it, in one of her now-familiar colloquialisms, "You betcha."

She was a political novice who lacked the intellectual heft necessary to occupy a place in the Beltway's corridors of power . . . or she was a commonsense, plain-speaking breath of fresh air who could shake Washington out of its deep doldrums and callous cynicism.

She was a religiously fundamentalist loon who probably handled snakes under cover of darkness . . . or she was a woman of deep, reasoned Christian faith who—like the vast majority of Americans—called upon bedrock spiritual beliefs to anchor her life and provide a moral compass.

She was a tough-love mom who ran a tight ship at home . . . or she was an out-of-touch mother who deserved most of the blame for her teen daughter's pregnancy that came to light in the early days of the '08 campaign.

She was a role model for women in America and in the world, standing for all that they aspire to become . . . or she was merely a cardboard feminist, standing for Stone Age subservience to men.

She was this, or she was that—but she was rarely anything in between.

At her party's national convention, when Palin joked about the difference between a hockey mom and a pit bull (punch line: lipstick), her fans cheered lustily while her opponents scoffed. When she appeared on *Saturday Night Live* and played along to comedienne Tina Fey's spot-on impersonation of her, Palin further displayed her penchant for self-deprecation and lightheartedness.

After the Republican ticket lost its bid for the White House, Palin became the source of rampant speculation about her political future. Her profile grew even larger when she unexpectedly resigned as governor and then joined Fox News Channel as a political commentator. By the time she rhetorically asked a gathering of Tea Party enthusiasts in early 2010, "How's that hopey-changey stuff workin' out for ya?" a sizeable "Palin for President" contingent had formed.

That not-so-subtle dig at President Barack Obama's administration certainly wasn't the first time Palin had said or written words that drew widespread attention. Although she is known more for her folksiness than for her scholarship, Palin has articulated thoughtful stands on a number of issues—often speaking or writing about them in her blog, on Facebook and Twitter, on Fox News, and in her best-selling book.

Going Rogue: An American Life hit bookshelves in November 2009 and was a huge success out of the gate, selling more than a million copies in the first two weeks. The title was inspired by the strong-willed reputation Palin gained within the McCain campaign. When she discussed the book on *The Oprah Winfrey Show*, the result was Oprah's highest rating in two years—about 8.7 percent of U.S. households, according to the *New York Times*. (A second Palin book, *America By Heart: Reflections on Family, Faith and Flag*, followed in the fall of 2010.)

Even so, with the mainstream press focusing largely on more shallow or tabloid-friendly fare (her accent, her looks, her parenting, her churchgoing habits), the vast majority of Palin's opinions and statements remain unfamiliar. That's where *The Quotable Rogue* comes in. From abortion to the Alaskan pipeline, from Wasilla to Washington, this compendium sets out to capture Palin's exact words on a range of important subjects.

No matter what the future holds for the moose-hunting hockey mom who emerged out of the dark and snowy Northwest on that August afternoon in 2008, Sarah Palin has already made an indelible mark—a mark that seems all the more indelible when examined in light of the thoughts she has expressed along the way.

ON ABORTION

I think it [abortion] should be a states' issue, not a federal government-mandated, mandating "yes" or "no" on such an important issue. I'm, in that sense, a federalist, where I believe that states should have more say in the laws of their lands and individual areas. Now, foundationally, it's no secret that I'm pro-life, that I believe in a culture of life, which is very important for this country. Personally that's what I would like to see further embraced by America.

—INTERVIEW WITH CBS'S KATIE COURIC, OCTOBER 1, 2008

I'm pro-life. I'll do all I can to see that every baby is created with a future and potential. The legislature should do all it can to protect human life.

—Q&A WITH NEWSMAX.COM'S MIKE COPPOCK, AUGUST 29, 2008

There are others [U.S. senators] that need to be moved quickly into the private sector, they are the foot soldiers in the Senate for this president who passed this health care bill who made us look complicit in all these abortions.

—SPEECH AT THE SUSAN B. ANTHONY LIST CELEBRATION OF LIFE BREAKFAST, *ALBANY TIMES-UNION*, MAY 14, 2010

Let's simplify, we're pro children.

—AT THE WISCONSIN RIGHT TO LIFE EDUCATION FUND, *MILWAUKEE JOURNAL SENTINEL*, NOVEMBER 6, 2009

I am and have always been unapologetically pro-life. What we thought was one of life's greatest challenges turned out to be one of life's greatest blessings . . . I feel blessed that God entrusted this opportunity to us.

—PALIN, REFERRING TO THE BIRTH OF HER SON TRIG, BORN WITH DOWN SYNDROME, *DAILY TEXAN*, APRIL 30, 2010

I have to be really careful in how I explain my feelings because some people say, "Oh, she considered abortion and how can that validate her pro-life position?" No, what Bristol [her daughter] and I have been through has not changed my belief, but it has changed my perspective on the whole situation.

—COMMENTING ON WHAT HER THOUGHTS WERE UPON FINDING OUT HER TEENAGE DAUGHTER WAS PREGNANT, *ARIZONA DAILY STAR*, MAY 15, 2010

I would like to see more women given more support so that those of us who say, "You know, a culture of life is what we believe," is best . . . for humankind, you know, to respect the sanctity of every human life. And to understand . . . that we live in a pretty messed-up world sometimes . . . The most promising and good ingredients in this world . . . is a child. The hope that a child brings. . . . I want to do all that I can to reduce the number of abortions [and] to usher in that culture of life. . . . [T]he common goal we have . . . is to see fewer and fewer abortions. And to provide more and more women support in this world.

—CBS, SEPTEMBER 30, 2008

I am pro-life. With the exception of a doctor's determination that the mother's life would end if the pregnancy continued. I believe that no matter what mistakes we make as a society, we cannot condone ending another life.

—Eagle Forum 2006 Gubernatorial Candidate
Questionnaire, July 31, 2006

Our prominent woman sisterhood is telling these young women that they are strong enough to deal with this . . . They can give their child life in addition to pursuing career and education and avocations. Society wants to tell these young women otherwise. These feminist groups want to tell these women that, "No, you're not capable of doing both." . . . It's very hypocritical.

—*Washington Post*, May 15, 2010

I am a normal American. And when it comes to my pro-life views, there are more Americans today saying that they understand the sanctity of life and that they are pro-life than they are pro-abortion for the first time in decades.

—*The O'Reilly Factor*, November 19, 2009

ON THE REAL AMERICA

What makes America exceptional isn't her politicians; it's her people.

—Examiner (Independence, MO), May 1, 2010

I grew up with those people [from small towns]. They are the ones who do some of the hardest work in America . . . who grow our food, run our factories, and fight our wars. They love their country in good times and bad, and they're always proud of America. I had the privilege of living most of my life in a small town.

—Republican National Convention speech in
Minneapolis, September 3, 2008

We believe that the best of America is not all in Washington, D.C. . . . We believe that the best of America is in these small towns that we get to visit, and in these wonderful little pockets of what I call the Real America, being here with all of you hardworking, very patriotic, very pro-America areas of this great nation.

—SPEAKING AT A FUND-RAISER IN GREENSBORO, NORTH CAROLINA, OCTOBER 16, 2008

CNN INTERVIEWER: You've talked about America. And certain parts of America, that are maybe more American than other parts of America. Are there?

SARAH PALIN: I don't want that misunderstood . . . You know, when I go to these rallies and we see the patriotism just shining through these people's faces and the Vietnam veterans wearing their hats so proudly, and they have tears in their eyes as we sing our national anthem, and it is so inspiring . . . I say that this is true America. You get it; you understand how important it is that in the next four years we have a leader who will fight for you. I certainly don't want that interpreted as one area being more patriotic or more American than another. If that's the way it's come across, I apologize.

—INTERVIEW WITH CNN'S DREW GRIFFIN, OCTOBER 21, 2008

You don't need a title to make a difference. Any ordinary American can seize opportunities to let their voice be heard . . . and they can make a difference.

—*Philadelphia Inquirer*, November 17, 2009

The people of America realize that all political power is inherent in the people. And government is to be implemented on behalf of the people and the will that they desire that their government engage in. You can't underestimate the wisdom of the people of America. They're seeing through the rhetoric, and they're seeing through a lot of the political cheap shots, also. And they're getting down to the facts and the voting records that are going to show that stark contrast.

—*Hannity & Colmes*, September 17, 2008

And we believe that the best of America is not all gathered in Washington D.C. We believe that it is here, in the kindness and the goodness and the courage of everyday, hardworking Americans— those of you who run our factories and grow our food and teach our children and fight our wars; this is where the goodness of America is.

—*Southeast Missourian*, October 30, 2008

We grow good people
in our small towns,
with honesty and
sincerity and dignity.

—REPUBLICAN NATIONAL CONVENTION SPEECH IN
MINNEAPOLIS, SEPTEMBER 3, 2008

ON LIVING
IN ALASKA

"We hunt as much as we can, and I'm proud to say our freezer
is full of wild game that we harvested here in Alaska."
Palin's favorite food? "Moose stew after a day of snow-
machining."

—Q&A WITH *NEWSWEEK*'S BRIAN BRAIKER, AUGUST 29, 2008

---

*A changing environment will affect Alaska more than
any other state because of our location. I'm not one,
though, who would attribute it to being man-made.*

—*NEWSMAX.COM*, AUGUST 2008

And Alaska—we're set up, unlike other states in the [U]nion,
where it's collectively that Alaskans own the resources. So we
share in the wealth when the development of these resources
occurs . . . It's to maximize benefits for Alaskans, not an individual
company, not some multinational somewhere, but for Alaskans.

—ON WHY SHE IMPOSED A WINDFALL PROFITS TAX ON THE OIL INDUSTRY IN
ALASKA AS A MECHANISM FOR ENSURING THAT ALASKANS SHARE IN THE
WEALTH GENERATED BY OIL COMPANIES, *NEW YORKER*, NOVEMBER 3, 2008

Well, it certainly does [give me foreign policy experience]
because our next-door neighbors are foreign countries.
They're in the state that I am the executive of. And there
in Russia . . . We have trade missions back and forth. It's
very important when you consider even national security
issues with Russia as Putin rears his head and comes into
the airspace of the United States of America; where do they
go? It's Alaska. It's just right over the border. It is from
Alaska that we send those out to make sure that an eye is
being kept on this very powerful nation, Russia, because
they are right there. They are right next to our state.

—EXPLAINING TO CBS'S KATIE COURIC WHY ALASKA'S PROXIMITY TO
RUSSIA GIVES HER FOREIGN POLICY EXPERIENCE, SEPTEMBER 24, 2008

And our congressional delegation . . . They do a great job for
us. Representative Don Young, especially—God bless him—with
transportation—Alaska did so well under the very basic provisions
of the transportation act that he wrote just a couple of years ago.
We had a nice bump there. We're very, very fortunate to receive the
largesse that Don Young was able to put together for Alaska.

—NATIONAL PUBLIC RADIO, SEPTEMBER 4, 2008

[Alaska is] small-town America. It's just good, unpre-
tentious, hardworking people who love their state, they
love their country, also proud to be American—the best
upbringing that I could have ever hoped for. My parents
instill[ed] in me not just a love of family and community, but a love of freedom and independence. That's what
growing up in Alaska has been about.

—*HANNITY & COLMES*, SEPTEMBER 17, 2008

I was raised in a family where gender was not going
to be an issue. The girls did what the boys did.
Apparently in Alaska that's quite commonplace.

—*TIMES* [U.K.], AUGUST 31, 2008

It is tragic that so many Alaska fishermen and their families have had their lives put on hold waiting for this decision. My heart goes out to those affected, especially the families of the thousands of Alaskans who passed away while waiting for justice.

—Commenting on the U.S. Supreme Court reducing the $2.5 billion punitive damages award in the Exxon Valdez oil spill case to no more than $507.5 million, *LegalNewsline*.com, September 10, 2008

———

In the past, Alaska's reputation didn't lead the rest of America to believe we were adamant about safe, clean, responsible development here. I say that because we had legislators who are now serving prison time, because they were found guilty of being corrupted for their votes on oil and gas taxes by oil and gas industry players. That reputation has really hurt Alaska, and it's no wonder that some have not wanted to believe that we are opening a new chapter in Alaska's life.

—*Investor's Business Daily*, July 11, 2008

———

I would think we all tear up during the national anthem at the beginning of a baseball game, don't we? That's an alikeness between Alaskans and New Yorkers.

—*Esquire*, March 2009

———

Oh, baby!

—Announcing that the amount of the Alaska Permanent Fund Dividend was $1,654 for each resident that year. This money comes from investment profits generated by the state's $39 billion oil-wealth savings account, *Anchorage Daily News*, September 19, 2007

[My family] is a microcosm of so much of Alaska. My husband is a commercial fisherman. He also works up in the north slopes in the oil fields. I'm the first female governor in Alaska, so that's brought with it kind of a whole new chapter in Alaska's life. Like my husband—up here they refer to him as the "first dude," not the first gentleman. And Todd . . . is such a dude. He's a four-time winner of the Iron Dog snow machine race, which is the world's longest and they say toughest snow machine race, 2,000 miles across Alaska. [It's a] whole new chapter here when Todd is asked to do things like—and he graciously complies and he has a good time doing it—hosting . . . the former first ladies' tea party. And he does just great at things like that, as well as working in oil fields, with snow machines and in commercial fishing. That's a dynamic here that's of interest to others. Again, sort of a microcosm . . . reflective of an Alaskan lifestyle that so many of us participate in.

—*Time*, August 29, 2008

ON THE GOODNESS
OF AMERICANS

There is one America, but there are different priorities reflected in individual Americans . . . I'll give you an example. [For some] people, money . . . and power, prestige, a title next to their name is the be-all, end-all. Other people, the highest priority would be their character, their reputation, their word, and money has nothing to do with that. The beauty of America is that individuals making up this great country do have different priorities.

—*Esquire*, March 2009

We need to spend more time lifting up America instead
of apologizing for the greatest country on earth.

—CBSNews.com, February 17, 2010

We see America as the greatest force for good in this
world. [We] can be that beacon of light and hope for
others who seek freedom and democracy.

—*New York Times*, October 4, 2008

SEAN HANNITY: What do you view—and I know this
came up in your interview with Charlie Gibson, as
it relates to the Bush Doctrine. What do you view as
the Bush Doctrine and what do you view as America's
role in the world? What is our role as a country, as it
relates to national security?

SARAH PALIN: That's a great question, and being an
optimist, I see our role in the world as one of being
a force for good and one of being the leader of the
world when it comes to the values that it seems that
humankind embraces—the values that encompass
life and liberty and the pursuit of happiness. And
that's not just in America; that is in our world.

And America is in a position, because we care for so many people, to be able to lead and to be able to have a strong diplomacy and a strong military. Also at the same time to defend not only our freedoms but, to help these rising, smaller democratic countries that are just . . . putting themselves on the map right now, and they're going to be looking to America as that leader.

—*Hannity & Colmes*, September 17, 2008

ON BARACK OBAMA

We're probably better off simply changing administrations.
So, folks, let's start the task in November, and what we start
in November 2010 let's finish it off in November 2012.

—WKTR-TV (NORFOLK, VA), JUNE 27, 2010

It's unbelievable. Unbelievable. No administration in America's
history would, I think, ever have considered such a step that we just
found out President Obama is supporting today. It's kinda like getting
out there on a playground, a bunch of kids, getting ready to fight,
and one of the kids saying, "Go ahead, punch me in the face, and I'm
not going to retaliate. Go ahead and do what you want to with me."

—PALIN COMMENTS ON PRESIDENT OBAMA PUTTING LIMITS ON THE USE
OF U.S. NUCLEAR WEAPONS, *THE SEAN HANNITY SHOW*, APRIL 7, 2010

This is a man [Barack Obama] who can give an entire speech about the wars America is fighting, and never use the word *victory* except when he's talking about his own campaign. But when the cloud of rhetoric has passed . . . when the roar of the crowd fades away . . . when the stadium lights go out, and those Styrofoam Greek columns are hauled back to some studio lot—what exactly is our opponent's plan? What does he actually seek to accomplish, after he's done turning back the waters and healing the planet? The answer is to make government bigger . . . take more of your money . . . give you more orders from Washington . . . and to reduce the strength of America in a dangerous world. America needs more energy . . . our opponent is against producing it.

—Republican National Convention speech in
Minneapolis, September 3, 2008

Treating this like a mere law enforcement matter places our country at grave risk, because that's not how radical Islamic extremists are looking at this. They know we're at war. And to win that war, we need a commander in chief, not a professor of law standing at the lectern.

—Criticizing Obama's handling of terrorism threats,
specifically the questioning by officials of the suspect in the
attempted Christmas Day bombing of a Northwest Airlines
flight to Detroit, Bloomberg, February 6, 2010

Do they think, really, that we're getting anything in return for all this bowing and kowtowing and apologizing? No, we don't get anything positive in return for this. So while President Obama is getting pushed around by the likes of Russia and China, our allies are left to wonder about the value of an alliance with our country any more. They're asking, what is it worth[?]

—ASSOCIATED PRESS, JUNE 28, 2010

How's that hopey-changey thing workin' out for you?

—*NEW YORK TIMES*, FEBRUARY 7, 2010

He sees a country that has to be apologized for around the world, especially to dictators. We want to be a dominant superpower. It's in America's best interest and the world's that we are.

—*VIRGINIAN-PILOT*, JUNE 28, 2010

I think if the election were today, I do not think Obama would be re-elected . . . He's not going to win if he continues on the path that he has America on today . . . There are many things that he is doing today that cause an uneasiness in many, many Americans.

—*Washington Times*, February 8, 2010

———

Well, I was reading my copy of today's *New York Times*, and I was interested to read about Barack's friends from Chicago. Turns out one of Barack's earliest supporters is a man who, according to the *New York Times*, and they are hardly ever wrong, was a domestic terrorist and part of a group that, quote, launched a campaign of bombings that would target the Pentagon and U.S. Capitol. Wow. These are the same guys who think patriotism is paying higher taxes.

—*New York Times*, October 4, 2008

———

We need someone who can talk about the wars that America is fighting and isn't afraid to use the word "victory." Just once I would love to hear Barack Obama say he wants America to win.

—*Missourian*, October 30, 2008

———

Usually [it's] a no-brainer that the "R" is going to take the cake up here [in Alaska]. But this is a little bit different situation now with Obama's message resonating, even with Alaskans. That being change, a desire for not embracing the status quo and politics as usual. But something different, something dynamic and charismatic. That does resonate well, that message of Obama's.

—INTERVIEW, *KUDLOW & CO.*, AUGUST 1, 2008

I betcha I'd have more endurance [running a foot race against Obama]. My one claim to fame in my own little internal running circle is a sub-four [hour] marathon. It wasn't necessarily a good running time, but it proves I have the endurance within me to at least gut it out, and that is something. If you ever talk to my old coaches, they'd tell you, too. What I lacked in physical strength or skill I made up for in determination and endurance. So if it were a long race that required a lot of endurance, I'd win.

—UPI NEWSTRACK, JULY 2, 2009

There is no need for a fundamental transformation of America. No thank you, Mr. President, you can keep that change.

—*TULSA WORLD*, MARCH 13, 2010

It would be my honor to assist and support our new president and the new administration. And I speak for other Republicans, other Republican governors also, they being willing also to, again, seize this opportunity that we have to progress this nation together, a united front.

—Remarking on the newly elected President Obama, CNN, November 12, 2008

When he is up there and he is telling us basically, "I know best; my people here in the White House know best, and we are going to tell you that, yes, you do want this essentially nationalized health care system," and we're saying, "No, we don't." And the messages are not being received by Barack Obama. So I think instead of lecturing, he needs to stop, and he needs to listen on health care issues. On national security, this perceived lackadaisical approach that he has to dealing with the terrorists. We're saying that concerns us, and we're going to speak up about it, and please don't . . . try to make us feel like we need to just sit down, shut up, and accept what you're doing to us.

—Fox News Interview with Chris Wallace, February 7, 2010

RUSH LIMBAUGH: This is an attempt by the media to make you stop being who you are. What it means is, they're really worried about the effectiveness that you have.

SARAH PALIN: Well, yeah, I guess that message is they do want me to sit down and shut up. But that's not going to happen. I care too much about this great country. Now, yes, speaking of some of those associations—and you're right; mainstream media is not holding Barack Obama accountable—let's talk quickly about ACORN [the Association of Community Organizations for Reform Now] and the unconscionable situation that we're facing right now with voter fraud. And given the ties between Obama and ACORN and the money that his campaign has sent them and the job that he had with them in the past, Obama has a responsibility to rein in ACORN and prove that he's willing to fight voter fraud. We called him on it.

—*The Rush Limbaugh Show*, October 14, 2008

By the way, these athletes can outperform many of us, and we should be proud of them. I hope President Obama's comments do not reflect how he truly feels about the special needs community.

—Commenting on Obama's apology for remarks he made on *The Tonight Show* comparing his poor bowling scores to that of athletes in the Special Olympics, *Anchorage Daily News*, March 21, 2009

People have asked if I'd ever challenge him [Barack Obama] to
one-on-one because we both love basketball. But look, he towers
over me and I wouldn't be complaining about an unfair advantage
there, but maybe I'd do better playing H-O-R-S-E with him than
one-on-one. [H-O-R-S-E is a one-on-one game that allows players
to shoot set-up shots without interference from their opponent.]

—UPI NEWSTRACK, JULY 2, 2009

Let the kids be kids, let them have their friends come over,
let 'em hold on to that childhood despite the fact that they
are going to be in the public eye in more formal settings
and everything else. Bring spunk and life into the White
House. You do that via children being allowed to have fun
and just be who they are, and they are just going to have
a blast, so it's going to be good for the country also to see
that young life in the White House. I think it's going to
just brighten up our entire country. I look forward to that.

—ADVICE TO MICHELLE OBAMA ON BEING THE FIRST LADY,
CNN'S WOLF BLITZER, NOVEMBER 12, 2008

You get the impression that he is continually surprised
by the inability of various centralized government
agencies to get more involved and help solve problems.
His lack of executive experience might explain this.

—TALK RADIO NEWS SERVICE, MAY 28, 2010

ON BEING GOVERNOR OF ALASKA

*If you read the report, you will see that there was
nothing unlawful or unethical about replacing a
Cabinet member. You got to read the report.*

—Speaking from the campaign trail in Pittsburgh, Palin comments on
her firing Alaska's Public Safety Commissioner, Walt Monegan, while
she was governor, United Press International, October 11, 2008

*I'm very, very pleased to be cleared of any legal
wrongdoing . . . any hint of any kind of unethical activity
there. Very pleased to be cleared of any of that.*

—On allegations that she abused her power as governor in the Troopergate
scandal; conference call with Alaska reporters, October 12, 2008.

Only dead fish go with the flow.

—Explaining why she quit the governorship, *Huffington Post*, July 3, 2009

When I took my oath of office to serve as your Governor, remember, I swore to steadfastly and doggedly guard the interests of this great state like a grizzly with cubs, as a mother naturally guards her own. Alaska, as a statewide family, we've got to fight for each other, not against, and not let external, sensationalized distractions draw us off course. As an exciting year of unpredictable change begins, we, too, have our work cut out for us. And we're all in this together. Just like our musk ox, they circle up to protect their future when they are challenged. We've got to do the same."

—*Alaska Dispatch*, January 22, 2009

I want people to remember me as having always conducted the state's business in an upright and honest manner. I want them to understand that I put Alaska first in every decision I made.

—*ALASKA BUSINESS MONTHLY*, DECEMBER 4, 2008

I love my job, and I love Alaska, and it hurts to make this choice [to resign as governor], but I'm doing what's best for them. As I thought about this announcement that I would not seek reelection, I thought about how much fun other governors have as lame ducks. They maybe travel around their state, travel to other states, maybe take their overseas international trade missions . . . I'm not going to put Alaskans through that. I promised efficiencies and effectiveness. That's not how I'm wired. I'm not wired to operate under the same old politics as usual.

—*WASHINGTON POST*, JULY 4, 2009

I think God's will has to be done in unifying people and companies to get that gas line built, so pray for that.

—COMMENTING ON THE $30 BILLION NATIONAL GAS PIPELINE
PROJECT THAT SHE WANTED BUILT IN THE STATE, SPEAKING TO
STUDENTS AT THE WASILLA ASSEMBLY OF GOD, JUNE 2008

Not that a Zamboni blade isn't great—I love Zambonis. But should that be a higher priority than what the troopers need in their car?

—Commenting on the Alaska Senate's draft budget with $15,000 going to the Homer Hockey Association Alaska for a blade sharpener for a Zamboni machine, *Anchorage Daily News*, April 2, 2008

CHRIS WALLACE: Reagan, during his entire second term as governor of California, was a lame duck. Reagan in that second term was being sharply attacked by antiwar radicals. I can tell you, Ronald Reagan would never have quit.

SARAH PALIN: It's a big difference between just getting political pot shots fired your way. I can handle those. I get those. Shoot, I . . . got more of those this morning. So what? That doesn't matter. But when it adversely affected the people that I was serving, that's bull. And I wasn't going to put up with that. Again, millions of dollars; a paralyzed administration; my staff not knowing what they could do or say, because the adversaries were continuing to obstruct. No way. I love Alaska too much to put them through that.

So . . . I'm going to hand the reigns over to the lieutenant governor. He's as conservative as I am. He can progress our agenda—a common-sense conservative agenda for our state. And we can all get on with life.

—Fox News interview with Chris Wallace, February 7, 2010

TIME: What has been your crowning achievement in office so far?

SARAH PALIN: We have protected our state sovereignty by taking on the big oil industry interests, making sure that there is not going to be any undue influence . . . [O]ur state administration and our state lawmakers will be making the decisions . . . based on sound, solid, unbiased information, not being corrupted by, in the case that I'm speaking of now, [an] oil service company's undue influence that has corrupted some lawmakers . . . And we have allowed measures to be put in place now where we can prove very, very sound and strict oversight of oil and gas development so that we can prove to the rest of the nation that we are ready, willing[,] and we are able to safely develop our resources. So that Alaska can be contributors, we can be producers, so we don't have to be takers from federal government but can be supplying the rest of the U.S. with American resources finally.

—*TIME*, AUGUST 29, 2008

It may be tempting and more comfortable to just keep your head down, plod along, and appease those who demand, "Sit down and shut up," but that's the worthless, easy path; that's a quitter's way out.

—ANNOUNCING HER RESIGNATION AS GOVERNOR, JULY 3, 2009

*If the criticism is that I cheer for my hometown team too often,
I'm going to be cheering for my kids' teams. The numbers speak for
themselves in the budget. People can take me at my word or not,
that I am not biased towards or against any region in Alaska.*

—ON PALIN'S BIG BUDGET CUTS TO THE CAPITAL BUDGET EXCEPT
ONE ITEM: A $630,000 APPROPRIATION TO THE WASILLA SPORTS
COMPLEX, *ANCHORAGE DAILY NEWS*, DECEMBER 7, 2007

---

*We've got to make sure the rest of the United States doesn't believe the
only thing going on in Alaska is FBI probes and corruption trials.*

—*ANCHORAGE DAILY NEWS*, DECEMBER 27, 2007

---

*How sad that Washington and the media will never understand
that it's about country. And though it's honorable for countless
others to leave their positions for a higher calling and without
finishing a term—of course we know them by now—for some
reason a different standard applies to the decisions I make.*

—*SEATTLE TIMES*, JULY 4, 2009

ON BEING SARAH

I may not answer the questions that either the moderator or you want to hear, but I'm going to talk straight to the American people and let them know my track record also.

—ON NOT ANSWERING QUESTIONS IN THE VICE PRESIDENTIAL DEBATE, ST. LOUIS, MISSOURI, OCTOBER 2, 2008

KATIE COURIC: What's your favorite movie and why?
SARAH PALIN: I love those old sports movies, like *Hoosiers*, and *Rudy*, those that show that the underdog can make it, and it's all about tenacity and work ethic and determination, and just doing the right thing.

—INTERVIEW WITH CBS's KATIE COURIC, OCTOBER 1, 2008

Everything I ever needed to know, I learned on the basketball court: self-discipline, setting goals, teamwork, responsibility . . . and faith.

—CHICAGO SUN-TIMES, MAY 13, 2010

The difference between a hockey mom and a pit bull? Lipstick.

—REPUBLICAN NATIONAL CONVENTION SPEECH IN MINNEAPOLIS, SEPTEMBER 3, 2008

I eat granola. I just happen to shoot and catch my organic food before I eat it . . . Here I am in Track Town USA and my kid's name is Track. How Eugene hippie can that be?

—AT THE LANE COUNTY REPUBLICAN'S LINCOLN DINNER, EUGENE, OREGON, KVAL NEWS, APRIL 24, 2010

[My father] would come home at night, there at the dinner
table. His hands would be just full of notes for the next day.
I take notes today, even on the palm of my hand. And just to
get the left all wee-wee'd up and get their heads spinning,
I'm going to promise that I'm going to keep doing it.

—Responding to criticism about writing notes on her hand, and poking fun
at Barack Obama's comment about Washington DC politicians getting all
"wee-wee'd" up about the health-care debate *Politico.com*, March 3, 2010

My dad always says, "Don't retreat, just reload." Don't
let anybody tell you to sit down and shut up.

—*Kansas City Star*, May 1, 2010

I was being interviewed on the [campaign] trail, and was
asked what I thought about the campaign closing up in
Michigan. I said, "I wish we were staying here"—that's
when I got a reputation of going rogue . . . Michigan has
always been near and dear to my heart, and the state I
went rogue in . . . Why would anyone give up in Michigan?

—*South Bend Tribune*, May 14. 2010

If the election had turned out differently, I could be the one overseeing the signing of bailout checks and Vice President Biden could be on the road selling his book Going Rogaine.

—CHRISTIAN SCIENCE MONITOR, DECEMBER 6, 2009

I don't like to shop.

—REFERRING TO THE WARDROBE PROVIDED FOR HER TO WEAR DURING THE PRESIDENTIAL ELECTION, *THE HILL*, NOVEMBER 17, 2009

I can't imagine where I'd be without the opportunities provided to me in sports. Sports taught me that gender isn't an issue; in fact, when people talk about me being the first female governor, I'm a little absent from that discussion, because I've never thought of gender as an issue. In sports, you learn self-discipline, healthy competition, to be gracious in victory and defeat, and the importance of being part of a team and understanding what part you play on that team. You all work together to reach a goal, and I think all of those factors come into play in my role as governor.

ALASKA BUSINESS MONTHLY, DECEMBER 4, 2008

What's more of a challenge for me over the years, being in elected office, has been more the age issue rather than a gender issue. I've totally ignored the issues that have potentially been affecting me when it comes to gender because I was raised in a family where [it] wasn't going to be an issue. The girls did what the boys did . . . But the age issue I think was more significant in my career than the gender issue . . . I don't have 30 years of political experience under my belt . . . that's a good thing, that's a healthy thing. That means my perspective is fresher, more in touch with the people I will be serving.

—TIME.COM, AUGUST 14, 2008

SEAN HANNITY: You obviously have a lot of passion. What motivates you? For example, what made you want to get into the political world? What made you so willing to accept this job and not blink? Where does your motivation come from?

SARAH PALIN: My love of this country. I'm one of those people, you know, I see a soldier walk through the airport and, my heart does a little double-take. And I hear the Pledge of Allegiance or our national anthem, and I get a lump in my throat. And I know that that's the majority of Americans. Also, I . . . have been so proud of our country, every step of the way. We've made mistakes. We learn from our mistakes.

—*HANNITY & COLMES*, SEPTEMBER 17, 2008

KATIE COURIC: Do you consider yourself a feminist?

SARAH PALIN: I do. I'm a feminist who believes in equal rights, and I believe that women certainly today have every opportunity that a man has to succeed and to try to do it all anyway. And I'm very, very thankful that I've been brought up in a family where gender hasn't been an issue. You know, I've been expected to do everything growing up that the boys were doing. We were out chopping wood and . . . hunting and fishing and filling our freezer with good, wild Alaskan game to feed our family. So it kinda started with that. With just that expectation that the boys and the girls in my community were expected to do the same and accomplish the same. That's just been instilled in me.

KATIE COURIC: What is your definition of a feminist?

SARAH PALIN: Someone who believes in equal rights. Someone who would not stand for oppression against women.

—Interview with CBS's Katie Couric, October 1, 2008

I would be perfectly happy to go back to Wasilla, Alaska, with my five children and my grandson and raise a happy, healthy family, loving our great outdoors, doing the things that we do in Alaska. But if I believe that in some capacity I can help this great nation, I'm going to be willing to sacrifice . . .

—The Glenn Beck Program, January 14, 2010

Hello. Thank you, Jay [Leno]. Thank you. I'm so happy to be here. This is a thrill of a lifetime really. And Alaska [is] so different from Los Angeles. Here when people have a frozen look on their face, I find out it's Botox. It is so beautiful here, though, so warm and beautiful. Back home . . . it was freezing. It was 5 degrees below Congress' approval rating.

—THE TONIGHT SHOW, MARCH 2, 2010

SARAH PALIN: I like running alone, and having the Secret Service with me added a little bit of pressure. I'm thinking I gotta have good form and can't be hyperventilating and can't be showing too much pain, and that adds a little more pressure on you as you're trying to be out there enjoying your run. Then I fell coming down a hill and was so stinkin' embarrassed that a golf cart full of Secret Service guys had to pull up beside me. My hands just got torn up, and I was dripping blood. In the debate you could see a big, fat, ugly Band-Aid on my right hand. I have a nice war wound now as a reminder of that fall in the palm of my right hand. For much of the campaign, shaking hands was a little bit painful.

RUNNER'S WORLD: I don't remember news reports about it.

SARAH PALIN: Heck no! I made those guys swear to secrecy.

—RUNNER'S WORLD, AUGUST 2009

ON CIVIL RIGHTS

Q: Do you support the Alaska Supreme Court's ruling that spousal benefits for state employees should be given to same-sex couples?

A: No, I believe spousal benefits are reserved for married citizens as defined in our constitution.

—Eagle Forum 2006 Gubernatorial Candidate
Questionnaire, July 31, 2006

I don't support defining marriage as anything but between one man and one woman, and I think through nuances we can go round and round about what that actually means. I'm being as straight up with Americans as I can in my nonsupport for anything but a traditional definition of marriage.

—Vice presidential debate against Sen. Joe Biden, October 2, 2008

---

*In 1998, [Alaskan] voters defined marriage in a traditional way,
as between a man and a woman, and I think most people believed
that inherent in that vote was that benefits presently supplied
to couples would be exclusively supplied to married couples.*

—ALASKA BUSINESS MONTHLY, DECEMBER 4, 2006

I'm absolutely for equal pay for equal work. The Ledbetter
pay act—it was gonna turn into a boon for trial lawyers
who, I believe, could have taken advantage of women
who [would] allege discrimination many, many years
ago. Thankfully, there are laws on the books—there have
been since 1963—that no woman could be discriminated
against in the workplace in terms of anything, but especially in terms of pay. So, thankfully we have the laws on
the books and they better be enforced . . . There should
be no fear of a lawsuit prohibiting a woman from making
sure that the laws that are on the books today are enforced.
I know in a McCain-Palin administration we will not stand
for any measure that would result in a woman being paid
less than a man for equal work.

—COMMENTING ON THE LILLY LEDBETTER FAIR PAY ACT OF
2009, WHICH EXTENDS THE TIME ALLOWED IN FILING FOR EQUAL
PAY LAWSUITS, CBS NEWS, SEPTEMBER 30, 2008

I think Senator Clinton showed a lot of determination and stick-to-itiveness in her campaigns, and I have to respect that. I don't have to agree with all that she tried to push through and parts of her agenda. In fact, I don't agree with all of it. But there are some things that Hillary Clinton did that nobody can take away from her. And that is the 18 million cracks that she put there in that highest and hardest glass ceiling in America's political scene. She was able to affect that, and I respect that.

—*HANNITY & COLMES*, SEPTEMBER 17, 2008

SEAN HANNITY: Did you ban books? Did you try to ban books in the Alaska library? In the Wasilla Library?

SARAH PALIN: No. But I got a kick out of that one [question] also. No banned books. No desire to ban a book. That list of banned books . . . that included Harry Potter . . . had not even been written or published before I was in there.

HANNITY: It's false?

PALIN: False.

—*HANNITY & COLMES*, SEPTEMBER 17, 2008

WHEREAS, Juneteenth is an annual holiday commemorating the ending of slavery—the oldest celebration of its kind. Its roots go back to June 19, 1865, when Union soldiers arrived in Galveston, Texas[,] to announce the war's end and that all slaves were now free. That news took two and a half years after President Lincoln's Emancipation Proclamation, which had become official January 1, 1863.

WHEREAS, today, Juneteenth is a day, a week, and in some areas, a month that is set aside to celebrate African American freedom.

WHEREAS, in cities across the country, people of all races, nationalities, & religions are joining together to celebrate this extremely important historical event.

NOW, THEREFORE, I, Sarah Palin, Governor of the state of Alaska, do hereby proclaim June 21, 2008, as Juneteenth Day in Alaska, and encourage all Alaskans to reflect on the importance of this celebration, and encourage citizens to take part in the events taking place in your communities.

—ALASKA GOVERNOR'S OFFICE: PROCLAMATION, JUNE 17, 2008

We believe that we have no more judicial options to pursue. So we may disagree with . . . the rationale behind the ruling, but our responsibility is to proceed forward with the law and abide by the [C]onstitution.

—ON COMPLYING WITH AN ALASKA SUPREME COURT ORDER THAT OFFERS HEALTH AND RETIREE BENEFITS TO SAME-SEX PARTNERS OF STATE EMPLOYEES STARTING JANUARY 1, 2007, *ANCHORAGE DAILY NEWS*, DECEMBER 21, 2006

Yes, the explicit sex-ed programs will not find my support.

—DECLARING HER SUPPORT FOR ABSTINENCE-ONLY EDUCATION IN A QUESTIONNAIRE DURING HER 2006 GUBERNATORIAL RACE, POLITICO.COM, SEPTEMBER 1, 2008

But you are talking about, I think, a value here, what my position is on homosexuality and can you pray it away 'cause I think that was the title that was listed in that bulletin. And, you know, I don't know what prayers are worthy of being prayed. And I don't know what prayers are gonna be answered or not answered. But as for homosexuality, I am not going to judge Americans and the decisions that they make in their adult personal relationships.

I have one of my absolute best friends for the last 30 years who happens to be gay. And I love her dearly. And she is not my "gay friend." She is one of my best friends who happens to have made a choice that isn't a choice that I have made. But I am not gonna judge people. And I love America, where we are more tolerant than other countries are. And are more accepting of some of these choices that sometimes people want to believe reflects solely on an individual's values or not. Homosexuality, I am not gonna judge people.

—September 30, 2008

ON ECONOMICS

It's a ridiculous situation that we're finding ourselves in now with the IMF [International Monetary Fund] and our huge contributions from the U.S., when we're facing our own states that are financially upside down because of some of the mandates coming from the federal government, increasing costs on our states and on our small businesses. That so much of our U.S. dollar would go to bail out a socialized country that made poor decisions, didn't live within its means, allowed the population there in Greece to have this entitlement mentality where they thought government was going to take care of everything and pay all their bills. And here—it's our money going to bail them out?

—Protesting the bailout of Greece's economy with, in part, money from the U.S. through the IMF, *On the Record with Greta Van Susteren*, May 14, 2010

This is an exciting time for this state [of Alaska], but we are
committed to containing the enthusiasm when it comes to
spending. Government is not going to grow beyond its means.

—*Bond Buyer*, December 22, 2006

I am a conservative Republican, a firm believer in free
market capitalism. A free market system allows all parties
to compete, which ensures the best and most competitive
project emerges, and ensures a fair, democratic process.
I will communicate progress on gas line negotiations to
the public. My administration will pursue the plan that is
best for ALL Alaskans. All qualified and viable proposals
and applicants will be considered.

—Palin-Parnell campaign booklet: *New Energy for Alaska*, November 3, 2006

There is an inherent link between energy and prosperity and
energy and security and energy and freedom. It's a matter
of not having the political will and that's something that
must change, or our nation will become insolvent.

—*Peoria Journal*, April 19, 2010

I can't attest that every fund that's being offered the state in the stimulus package will be used to create jobs and stimulate the economy, so I'm requesting only those things that I know will. Public discussion will have to ensue on all those other dollars that some will say "you left on the table."

—PALIN EXPLAINING THAT SHE WOULD ACCEPT ONLY 69 PERCENT OF THE ESTIMATED $930 MILLION DOLLARS THAT COULD FLOW TO ALASKA FROM THE FEDERAL GOVERNMENT. SHE SAID THAT HER ACCEPTANCE WAS FOR MONEY THAT WAS "TIMELY, TARGETED AND TEMPORARY" WITHOUT STRINGS THAT BIND THE STATE IN THE FUTURE, AMERICA'S INTELLIGENCE WIRE, MARCH 20, 2009

Well, I killed the "bridge to nowhere." And you know, I think I ruffled some feathers there, also, with our congressman who had been requesting that bridge for so many years . . . What we needed to do up there in Alaska, was to find some good transportation between the two land bodies there. And we did. We found that with an improved ferry system between Ketchikan and its airport. But . . . Alaskans [are] not willing to support [it] to such an extent that we'll pay for it ourselves. We better kill the bridge, because we know the rest of the nation's not going to pay for it.

—COMMENTING ON A BRIDGE IN ALASKA THAT HAD BEEN FEDERALLY FUNDED AND WAS HELD UP AS AN EXAMPLE OF PORK BARREL SPENDING, *HANNITY & COLMES*, SEPTEMBER 17, 2008

The purchase of the jet was impractical and unwise, and it's time to get rid of it.

—On selling the governor's jet that had become a high-profile campaign issue in the Republican gubernatorial primary in which Palin beat incumbent Governor Frank Murkowski. She won the governorship in November, *Los Angeles Times*, December 12, 2006

While I was at it, I got rid of a few things in the governor's office that I didn't believe our citizens should have to pay for. That luxury jet was over-the-top. I put it on eBay. I also drive myself to work.

—Republican National Convention speech in Minneapolis, September 3, 2008

*As mayor, I took a voluntary pay cut, which didn't thrill my husband;
and then as governor I cut the personal chef position from the
budget, and that didn't thrill my hungry kids. And I put the state's
checkbook online for all to see, and that didn't thrill the bureaucrats.*

—BLOOMBERG, SEPTEMBER 15, 2008

---

*While lower crude oil prices are reducing the costs of
energy today, we must remain committed to achieving
energy security for our future economic well being.*

—BOND BUYER, JANUARY 30, 2009

ON CRIME

We are getting tough on criminals with tougher, defensible sentences. It was a clean sweep for convictions in the Cold Case Unit. Our Civil Division is managing hundreds of legal battles to protect Alaskans' interests. I commend Law for last year's needed, comprehensive ethics bill. In Military and Veterans Affairs, we certified hundreds of territorial guardsmen, so those who served finally receive their benefits. We are proudly supporting our brave Alaska Guard as they provide daily search and rescue in our State, and support the War on Terror.

—2008 State of the State Address to 25th
Alaska Legislature, January 15, 2008

I support adequate funding for a strong public safety presence in Alaska. Feeling safe in our communities is something we cannot accept any compromise on. This includes policing in all its forms, the court system, prosecutors and corrections. If the legislature passed a death penalty law, I would sign it. We have a right to know that someone who rapes and murders a child or kills an innocent person in a drive-by shooting will never be able to do that again.

—WWW.PALINFORGOVERNOR.COM, *ISSUES*, NOVEMBER 7, 2006

I can't claim a Bill Clinton and say that I never inhaled.

—ON SMOKING MARIJUANA, WHICH WAS LEGAL UNDER ALASKA LAW. LATER IN THE ARTICLE, SHE SAID SHE DIDN'T LIKE IT AND DOESN'T SMOKE IT NOW, *ANCHORAGE DAILY NEWS*, AUGUST 6, 2006

*If we're talking about pot, I'm not for the legalization of pot. I think
that would just encourage our young people to think that it was
OK to go ahead and use it. However, I think we need to prioritize
our law enforcement efforts. If somebody's gonna smoke a joint
in their house and not do anybody any harm, then perhaps there
are other things our cops should be looking at to engage in and
try to clean up some of the other problems we have in society.*

—POLITICO.COM, JUNE 17, 2010

Q: Will you support an effort to expand hate-crime laws?

A: No, as I believe all heinous crime is based on hate.

Q: Do you support the expansion of gambling in Alaska?

A: No, in so many cases, gambling has shown ill effects
on families and as governor I would not propose
expansion legislation.

Q: Would you sign any bills that expand gaming in our
state?

A: No.

—EAGLE FORUM 2006 GUBERNATORIAL CANDIDATE
QUESTIONNAIRE, JULY 31, 2006

My family and I are thankful that the jury thoroughly and carefully weighed the evidence and issued a just verdict. Besides the obvious invasion of privacy and security concerns surrounding this issue, many of us are concerned about the integrity of our country's political elections. America's elections depend upon fair competition. Violating the law, or simply invading someone's privacy for political gain, has long been repugnant to Americans' sense of fair play. As Watergate taught us, we rightfully reject illegally breaking into candidates' private communications for political intrigue in an attempt to derail an election.

—Reaction to a college student accused of hacking into Palin's e-mail account. The student was convicted on two counts of destroying records and unlawful access to a computer, *PC Magazine Online*, April 30, 2010

ON EDUCATION

Q: Will you support the right of parents to opt out their children from curricula, books, classes, or surveys, which parents consider privacy-invading or offensive to their religion or conscience?

A: Yes. Parents should have the ultimate control over what their children are taught.

—EAGLE FORUM 2006 GUBERNATORIAL CANDIDATE
QUESTIONNAIRE, JULY 31, 2006

We're not educating our youth about the exceptional nature of America. For America to survive, we've got to pass that on to the next generation.

—LOS ANGELES TIMES, JUNE 26, 2010

Q: Did you only want to teach creationism in school and not evolution?

A: No. In fact, growing up in a schoolteacher's house with a science teacher as a dad, I have great respect for science being taught in our science classes and evolution to be taught in our science classes.

—*HANNITY & COLMES*, SEPTEMBER 17, 2008

You mentioned education, and I'm glad you did . . . America needs to be putting a lot more focus on that and our schools have got to be really ramped up in terms of the funding that they are deserving. Teachers needed to be paid more. I come from a house full of schoolteachers. We have got to increase the standards. No Child Left Behind was implemented. It's not doing the job though. We need flexibility in No Child Left Behind. We need to put more of an emphasis on the profession of teaching. My kids are public school participants right now, and it's near and dear to my heart.

—2008 VICE PRESIDENTIAL DEBATE AGAINST JOE BIDEN, OCTOBER 2, 2008

It is our energy development that pays for essential services, like education. Victor Hugo said, "He who opens a school door, closes a prison." It's a privileged obligation we have to "open education doors." Every child, of every ability, is to be cherished and loved and taught. Every child provides this world hope. They are the most beautiful ingredient in our sometimes muddied-up world. I am committed to our children and their education. Stepping through "the door" is about more than passing a standardized test. We need kids prepared to pass life's tests—like getting a job and valuing a strong work ethic. Our Three-year Education Plan invests more than a billion dollars each year. We must forward-fund education, letting schools plan ahead. We must stop pink-slipping teachers, and then struggle to recruit and retain them the next year.

—2008 State of the State Address, January 15, 2008

We'll fully forward-fund all our school districts with more than a billion dollars—that's more than 21 percent of General Fund expenditures. Education is that high a priority. We'll focus on early learning, vo-tech [vocational technology] and workforce development, an enhanced University, streamlined operations, we'll hold schools accountable, and we'll encourage opportunities for students with special needs.

—Alaska 2009 State of the State Address, January 22, 2009

We have no needs-based aid for Alaska students. Governor Murkowski tried to put $20 million in the budget for aid, but the Legislature rejected it. Let's make our own University available to students who might otherwise go without higher education . . . The State should target early education programs to specific at-risk groups that truly need them. These groups will benefit from access to high-quality programs currently out of their reach. We must find a way for these children to obtain a safe and positive environment in their early years. Today, social and economic pressures sometimes encourage both parents to return to work outside the home. My administration will publish useful educational material for parents about children in their early years.

—PALIN-PARNELL CAMPAIGN BOOKLET: *NEW ENERGY FOR ALASKA*, NOVEMBER 3, 2006

It's OK to let kids know that there are theories out there. They gain information just by being in a discussion . . . My dad did talk a lot about his theories of evolution. He would show us fossils and say, "How old do you think these are?" . . . I believe we have a creator. I'm not going to pretend I know how all this came to be.

—FOLLOW-UP ON ALASKA 2006 GOVERNOR DEBATE:
ANCHORAGE DAILY NEWS, OCTOBER 27, 2006

ON ENERGY POLICY

What I can do, [as governor] specifically, in helping our nation become energy independent, of course, comes from my experience as an oil and gas regulator in a huge energy-producing state and now as governor of that state. We know that we have the domestic solutions and the domestic supplies of energy. And we have the American ingenuity, and we have the American workers ready to be put to use to allow our nation to become less dependent on foreign sources of energy, volatile foreign regimes that control too much of our energy supply and use energy as a weapon. We need to get away from that. And domestic solutions that are at our fingertips—I want to help lead in that area.

—*Larry King Live*, November 12, 2008

Our focus is on recognizing and acknowledging that we need those green, clean sources of energy. But there's going to be a gap between now and when those sources of energy come online . . . so filling that gap has got to be the conventional sources of energy.

—NATURAL GAS WEEK, MARCH 3, 2008

JOE BIDEN: We're not going to support the $300 billion tax cut that they have for corporate America and the very wealthy. We're not going to support another $4 billion tax cut for ExxonMobil.

SARAH PALIN: Senator Biden, you would remember that, in that energy plan that Obama voted for, that's what gave those oil companies those big tax breaks. Your running mate voted for that. You know what I had to do in the state of Alaska? I had to take on those oil companies and tell them, "No," . . . that wasn't going to happen in my state. And that's why Exxon and ConocoPhillips, they're not my biggest fans, because what I had to do up there in Alaska was to break up a monopoly . . . and say, "You know, the people are going to come first, and we're going to make sure that we have value given to the people of Alaska with those resources."

—VICE-PRESIDENTIAL DEBATE AGAINST SEN. JOE BIDEN, OCTOBER 2, 2008

Oil and coal? Of course, it's a fungible commodity, and they don't flag . . . where it's going and where it's not. But in the sense of the Congress today, they know that there are very, very hungry domestic markets that need that oil first. So, I believe that what Congress is going to do . . . is not to allow the export bans to such a degree that it's Americans that get stuck to holding the bag without the energy source that is produced here, pumped here. It's got to flow into our domestic markets first.

—Speech in Grand Rapids, Michigan, September 17, 2008

Our opponents say, again and again, that drilling will not solve all of America's energy problems—as if we all didn't know that already. But the fact that drilling won't solve every problem is no excuse to do nothing at all . . . To confront the threat that Iran might seek to cut off nearly a fifth of world energy supplies . . . or that terrorists might strike again at the Abqaiq facility in Saudi Arabia . . . or that Venezuela might shut off its oil deliveries . . . we Americans need to produce more of our own oil and gas. And take it from a gal who knows the North Slope of Alaska: we've got lots of both.

—Republican National Convention speech in
Minneapolis, September 3, 2008

Windfall profits taxes alone [on oil companies] prevent additional investment in domestic production. Without new supplies from American reserves, our dependency and addiction to foreign sources of oil will continue.

—ALASKA GOVERNOR'S OFFICE: PRESS RELEASE,
OBAMA ENERGY PLAN, AUGUST 4, 2008

I'm pleased to report to Alaskans that in early August, our Alaska Legislature agreed to approve a one-time resource rebate that returns part of our resource wealth to Alaskans—the owners in common of these resources. The rebate will be a direct payment of $1,200 to each Alaskan eligible for the 2008 Permanent Fund Dividend. The resource rebate was part of a larger energy package that also includes a 50 percent increase in the maximum loan amount for bulk fuel bridge and bulk fuel revolving loan funds to communities and cooperatives. Additionally, it suspends the state's 8-cent motor fuel tax on gasoline, marine fuel and aviation fuel for one year and strengthens the Power Cost Equalization Program.

Our lawmakers also included an additional $60 million for the Home Energy Rebate Program operated by the Alaska Housing Finance Corporation and $50 million in grant funds to the Renewable Energy Fund, bringing the total available for renewable energy projects in FY 2009 to $100 million.

—ALASKA GOVERNOR'S OFFICE: AUGUST 2008 NEWSLETTER

*Certainly we need that [alterative energy], but he [Barack Obama]
is wrong not to acknowledge that we still need the conventional
sources of energy to be drilled here . . . Otherwise, we are going
to be dropped to our knees and bowing to the Saudis, Venezuela
and places like Russia that will keep producing oil and petroleum
products. Then we will have to ask them to produce for us because
we will still be dependent upon these sources of energy.*

—AFTER THE PRESIDENT'S SPEECH ON THE BP OIL SPILL,
NEW YORK DAILY NEWS, JUNE 16, 2010

When we talk about energy, we have to consider the need
to do all that we can to allow this nation to become energy
independent. It's a nonsensical position that we are in when
we have domestic supplies of energy all over this great
land. And East Coast politicians who don't allow energy-
producing states like Alaska to produce these, to tap into
them, and instead we're relying on foreign countries to
produce for us. We're circulating about $700 billion a year
into foreign countries, some who do not like America—they
certainly don't have our best interests at heart—instead of
those dollars circulating here, creating thousands of jobs
and allowing domestic supplies of energy to be tapped into
and start flowing into these very, very hungry markets.
Energy independence is the key to this nation's future, to
our economic future, and to our national security.

—2008 VICE PRESIDENTIAL DEBATE AGAINST SEN. JOE BIDEN, OCTOBER 2, 2008

This solidifies our commitment to facilitating an LNG [Liquid Natural Gas] project that is a product of market interest. By committing both project capital and natural gas resources to a pipeline that would transport North Slope natural gas to tidewater, an LNG project can remain an integral element of the state's effort to deliver Alaska's gas to market.

—On signing an order directing the state Department of Natural Resources and the Department of Revenue to work cooperatively with any organization or entity committed to commercializing Alaska's North Slope natural gas, Alaska Governor's Office: press release, *Admin. Order 242,* August 20, 2008

Q: When we talked about a month ago, you told me you were going to persuade Senator McCain to drill in ANWR [Arctic Natinal Wildlife Refuge]. Now actually, McCain's come a long way on drilling Outer Continental Shelf. Have you yet talked him in to ANWR?

A: I have not talked him in to ANWR yet. But yeah, he has evolved into being open enough to say yes to that offshore. Obama certainly hasn't gone there. We certainly need this. We need it for American security and for energy independence.

—*Kudlow & Co.,* July 31, 2008

*I don't see national energy policy as an either/or proposition.
Rather, we need to develop secure domestic sources of
conventional energy, such as oil and natural gas, while also
researching and developing alternative and renewable energy.*

—LETTER TO MEMBERS OF THE U.S. SENATE AND PRESIDENT
GEORGE W. BUSH, NOVEMBER 10, 2007

Q: The governor of Alaska sent a letter to Senate Leader
Harry Reid with a very clear demand—drill in ANWR
now. Governor Sarah Palin is on the phone right now.
Governor, I'm curious how you were received today,
when so many of your constituents, I would assume,
want to protect the land, not drill. How did it go today?

A: I'll correct you there with all due respect. The people
of Alaska understand that Alaska has so much to
contribute in terms of energy sources to the rest of
the U.S. Folks up here want ANWR to be unlocked by
the federal government so that we can drill. We've
got a tremendous amount of resource up here, and
we're ready, willing, and able to contribute. I think
Washington doesn't understand that we're at a real
critical crossroads: We are either going to become
more and more dependent on foreign sources of
energy, or we're going to be able to secure our nation
and drill domestically for safe, stable, clean supplies
of energy that we have here. We have them in Alaska.

—*YOUR WORLD WITH NEIL CAVUTO*, JUNE 27, 2008

Q: What specific role will you take on as vice president?

A: I will focus on energy independence. First and foremost, an energy-independent nation. We must get there. It is a matter of national security and of our future prosperity, being able to quit relying on foreign sources of energy to feed our hungry markets when we have the American supplies, and we have the American ingenuity, and we have the American workers to produce these supplies of energy.

Q: Americans have heard a lot of information on ANWR. I've heard you talk passionately about your love for your state of Alaska.

A: Yes.

Q: Why then would you support drilling in Alaska?

A: I support drilling in Alaska because it's going to be good for our nation.

Q: Including ANWR?

A: Absolutely. ANWR is a 2,000-acre plot of land. It's about the size of LAX [the official name of Los Angeles International Airport], that platform of land that we would need to explore. But, no secret, John McCain and I agree to disagree on that one. And I'm going to keep working on him with ANWR.

—*HANNITY & COLMES*, SEPTEMBER 17, 2008

President Bush is right. Across the nation, communities are feeling the pinch of high energy costs. It is absurd that we are borrowing from one foreign country to buy oil from another. It is a threat to our national security and economic well-being. It is well past time for America to develop our own supplies.

—AFTER PRESIDENT BUSH RENEWED HIS CALL TO OPEN THE ARCTIC NATIONAL WILDLIFE REFUGE FOR OIL EXPLORATION IN THE FACE OF SURGING GASOLINE PRICES, ALASKA GOVERNOR'S OFFICE: PRESS RELEASE 8-068, *ANWR*, APRIL 29, 2008

God has so richly blessed this land, not just with the oil and the gas, but with wind and the hydro, the geothermal and the biomass. We'll tap into those.

—SPEECH AT ELON UNIVERSITY DISCUSSING THAT SHE AND GOP PRESIDENTIAL NOMINEE JOHN MCCAIN WILL DEVELOP NEW ENERGY SOURCES, AS REPORTED IN THE *MEADVILLE TRIBUNE*, OCTOBER 16, 2008

CHARLIE GIBSON: When I asked John McCain about your national security credentials, he cited the fact that you have commanded the Alaskan National Guard and that Alaska is close to Russia. Are those sufficient credentials?

SARAH PALIN: Let me speak specifically about a credential that I do bring to this table, and that's with the energy independence that I've been working on for these years as the governor of this state that produces nearly 20 percent of the U.S. domestic supply of energy, that I worked on as chairman of the Alaska Oil and Gas Conservation Commission, overseeing the oil and gas development in our state to produce more for the United States.

CHARLIE GIBSON: I know. I'm just saying that national security is a whole lot more than energy.

SARAH PALIN: It is, but I want you to not lose sight of the fact that energy is a foundation of national security. It's that important. It's that significant.

—2008 ELECTION INTERVIEW WITH CHARLIE GIBSON, SEPTEMBER 11, 2008

We do have to drill. We cannot stall. We do need oil.

—CHICAGO TRIBUNE, MAY 12, 2010

We've got to tap domestically, because energy security will be the key to our prosperity . . . I want our country to be able to trust the oil industry.

—Speaking at the Independence Events Center, as reported in the *Kansas City Star*, May 1, 2010

What, on a real practical level here, the GOP has got to do, though, between now and the election, is to convince Americans that it is our energy policy that is best for our nation and the nation's future, that if we are to become energy independent and if we are to become a more secure nation then we had better start supplying our very, very hungry markets across the nation with American supplies of energy. And up here in Alaska we're sitting on billions of barrels of oil. We're sitting on hundreds of trillions of cubic feet of natural gas onshore and offshore. And it seems to be only the Republicans who understand that companies should be competing for the right to tap those resources, and get that energy source flowing into these hungry markets so that we will be less reliant on foreign sources of energy. In a volatile world, relying on foreign regimes that are not friendly to Americans, asking them to ramp up resource production for our benefit, that's nonsensical.

—*Time*, August 29, 2008

Alaskans have appreciated your strong support for construction of a pipeline. The project is now moving forward, and I believe that a discussion between you and Prime Minister Harper would greatly facilitate the process now under way.

—On pushing for a natural gas pipeline project from the North Slope of Alaska into Canada, as reported in the *Houston Chronicle*, February 7, 2009

We need to be doing everything, and people need to be realistic also. And this is also what kind of scares me about Biden and Obama also—it seems to be almost a naive notion of theirs that we can automatically just jump right into a renewable supply of energy to feed hungry markets across our nation when these renewables are not yet proven to be economic nor reliable. We're going to be in a transition period for quite some time where we're going to have to continue to be reliant on conventional sources of energy as we're working on the renewables, and we certainly have to head in that direction also. But it's got to be doing everything, everything that we can to allow the domestic supplies, renewable and nonrenewable, to be tapped, solutions plugged in from both those ends, and not just skip the oil and the gas development and the coal development also that we have to have as part of a comprehensive plan. It's naive to think we can go right to renewables and think that's ever going to work.

—Interview with Maria Bartiromo on CNBC, August 29, 2008

I am pleased to see Senator Obama acknowledge the huge potential Alaska's natural gas reserves represent in terms of clean energy and sound jobs. The steps taken by the Alaska State Legislature this past week demonstrate that we are ready, willing and able to supply the energy our nation needs.

—Politico.com, August 5, 2008

As John McCain has observed, for a guy's whose slogan is "Yes, we can," Barack Obama's energy plan sure has a whole lot of "No, we can't."

—Associated Press, October 30, 2008

ON THE
ENVIRONMENT

*These people have suffered long enough. While Exxon may have
the ability to delay payments, I strongly encourage them to bring
this sad chapter in our history to a long-overdue conclusion.
It is time to end the misery so everyone can move on.*

—Encouraging Exxon Mobil to pay the $507 million in punitive
damages plus interest awarded by the U.S. Supreme Court to 32,000
plaintiffs in the 1989 Exxon Valdez oil spill lawsuit, Alaska
Governor's Office: Press release 08-106, *Exxon*, July 1, 2008

When you ask Alaskans, "Do you agree to allow drilling
to take place on the North Slope," specifically here, we're
talking about ANWR, "Do you want to see that happen?"
And with Alaskans' love and care for our environment
and our lands and our wildlife, Alaskans are saying yes
because we believe that it can be done safely, prudently,

and it had better be done ethically also. Yes, we want to see that drilling. So hopefully the rest of America can understand that also. You go door-to door and ask Alaskans if we are ready and willing to produce more and contribute more to the U.S. and they're going to tell you yes.

—CNBC INTERVIEW WITH MARIA BARTIROMO, AUGUST 29, 2008

As governor of the nation's only Arctic state, Alaska feels and sees impacts of climate change more so than any other state. And we know that it's real. I'm not one to attribute every activity of man to the changes in the climate. There is something to be said also for man's activities, but also for the cyclical temperature changes on our planet. But there are real changes going on in our climate. And I don't want to argue about the causes. What I want to argue about is, how are we going to get there to positively affect the impacts? We have got to clean up this planet. We have got to encourage other nations also to come along with us.

—2008 VICE PRESIDENTIAL DEBATE AGAINST SEN. JOE BIDEN, OCTOBER 2, 2008

I'm not an Al Gore, doom-and-gloom environmentalist blaming the changes in our climate on human activity.

—HOUSTON CHRONICLE, SEPTEMBER 13, 2008

Q: What is your take on global warming and how is it affecting our country?

A: A changing environment will affect Alaska more than any other state, because of our location. I'm not one though who would attribute it to being man-made.

—Q&A WITH NEWSMAX.COM'S MIKE COPPOCK, AUGUST 29, 2008

You asked for the job, Mr. President, so buck up.
After two months of incompetence from the federal
government, they are taking it in their own hands.

—ON THE FEDERAL GOVERNMENT'S SLOW RESPONSE TO THE
BP OIL SPILL, ASSOCIATED PRESS, JUNE 27, 2010

I was the first governor to form a climate change sub-cabinet to start dealing with the impacts. We've got to reduce emissions. John McCain is right there with an "all of the above" approach to deal with climate change impacts. As we rely more on other countries that don't care as much about the climate as we do, we're allowing them to produce and to emit and even pollute more than America would ever stand for. It's all the more reason that we have an "all of the above" approach, tapping into alternative sources of energy and conserving fuel, conserving our petroleum products and our hydrocarbons so that we can clean up this planet.

—VICE PRESIDENTIAL DEBATE AGAINST SEN. JOE BIDEN, OCTOBER 2, 2008

We need to analyze the potential economic costs, needs and opportunities associated with climate change. Let's be cautious in how we react to make sure we don't overreact. The Alaska Climate Impact Assessment Commission is supposed to assess the situation and issue a report on March 1, 2007. This is a good start.

—2006 GUBERNATORIAL CANDIDATE PROFILE,
ANCHORAGE DAILY NEWS, OCTOBER 22, 2006

We believe that the Service's decision to list the polar bear [under the Endangered Species Act] was not based on the best scientific and commercial data available.

—GOVERNOR SARAH PALIN ANNOUNCING THAT THE STATE OF ALASKA FILED A LAWSUIT IN U.S. DISTRICT COURT FOR THE DISTRICT OF COLUMBIA, SEEKING TO OVERTURN INTERIOR SECRETARY DIRK KEMPTHORNE'S DECISION TO LIST THE POLAR BEAR AS THREATENED, ALASKA GOVERNOR'S OFFICE: PRESS RELEASE, *POLAR BEAR*, AUGUST 4, 2008

KATIE COURIC: I want to start with climate change, if I could. What's your position on global warming? Do you believe it's man-made or not?

SARAH PALIN: Well, we're the only Arctic state, of course, Alaska. So we feel the impacts more than any other state up there . . . And certainly it is apparent. We have erosion issues and we have melting sea ice, of course. So what I've done up there is form a sub-cabinet to focus solely on climate change. Understanding that it is real.

KATIE COURIC: Is it manmade in your opinion?

SARAH PALIN: I'm not going to solely blame all of man's activities on changes in climate. Because the world's weather patterns are cyclical, and over history we have seen changes there. But it kind of doesn't matter at this point, as we debate what caused it. The point is it's real, we need to do something about it. And like . . . Tony Blair had said . . . when he was in [a] leadership position, he said, "Let's all consider the fact that it is real." So instead of pointing fingers . . . at different sides of the argument as to who is to blame, and if nature is just to blame, let's do something about it. Let's clean up our world. Let's reduce emissions. And let's go with reality.

KATIE COURIC: Because, if it's not man-made, then one might wonder, well, how can human beings contribute to a solution?

SARAH PALIN: Well, human beings certainly are contributing to pollution today, and to some adverse effects on the environment. And it's all of our jobs to do to clean things up. And that's what we're committed to doing.

—Interview with CBS's Katie Couric, October 1, 2008

Our scientists feel confident that it would be unwarranted to list Cook Inlet belugas now. Seven years ago, NMFS determined that these whales weren't endangered, and since then, we've actually seen the beginnings of an increase in their population. We are all doing everything we can to help protect these important marine mammals.

I am especially concerned that an unnecessary federal listing [of beluga whales on the Endangered Species List] and designation of critical habitat would do serious long-term damage to the vibrant economy of the Cook Inlet area.

—Press release urging the National Marine Fisheries Service (NMFS) not to list the species, Alaska Governor's Office: Press release 07-175, *Beluga*, August 7, 2007

[BP is] looking out for their bottom line. Their interpretation of situations is so often a lot different than the public, the innocent public members who are adversely affected by a spill like what we're seeing going on in the Gulf. Sometimes their interpretation of the situation is a little bit different than what the average American is observing.

What we're observing now is that blame game, and that's not solving the problem. We've got to stop that leak, and we've got to keep from it coming ashore. And I say this as a pro-development, pro-drilling advocate, as somebody who lived and worked through the Exxon oil spill in Valdez, Alaska, 20-some years ago. Todd and I making our living on the water, commercial fishermen, we being forever adversely affected by that spill, knowing that Exxon at the time was going to claim that 150-year-old maritime law as protection against providing remedy to those who were adversely affected . . . we have to do what we did in Alaska, make the oil companies follow. Take them to court. Do litigation, whatever it takes. And through the court of public opinion, put pressure on the oil companies and hold them accountable for any lax in terms of preventive measures or any lax in maintenance that would allow such a tragedy to happen. We have to hold the oil companies accountable.

—*On the Record with Greta Van Susteren*, May 14, 2010

Let's look at lessons learned over the last 30 years when the Trans-Alaska oil pipeline was finally allowed to be built, and there were the threats then and the fears that the caribou herds would diminish and die off. No, the caribou herds are actually thriving. They're flourishing. There have not been the adverse impacts on the caribou herds, so we anticipate the same thing as we tap more energy supplies up on the north slope in ANWR and as we build a natural gas pipeline also that's under way at this point . . . that pipeline has supplied 15 billion barrels of oil into our domestic supplies here in America. And by the way, Joe Biden was one who voted against that Trans-Alaska oil pipeline 30 years ago. He was fearful of allowing ramped-up domestic supplies of foreign energy even then. So of course I fear that if he's of the same mind today, we're in a world of hurt there. No. The environment will continue to be protected. Our wildlife will continue to thrive and to prosper up there. And we're going to make sure that we have the stringent and safe oversight that is necessary and that will allow the population of this wildlife and the pristineness of the area to continue.

—CNBC MARIA BARTIROMO INTERVIEW, AUGUST 29, 2008

We are setting our standards high, but that's because the stakes are high for Alaska and for a nation that depends on our oil and gas.

—On establishing the Petroleum Systems Integrity Office under the Alaska Department of Natural Resources to provide state oversight of the entire pipeline process. The new office was created in response to "lax maintenance practices" on the North Slope after a transit pipe spilled more than 200,000 gallons of crude oil on the tundra, *Oil Daily*, April 19, 2007

ON FAMILY

Sometimes even the greatest joys bring challenge. And children with special needs inspire a special love . . . To the families of special-needs children all across this country, I have a message: For years, you sought to make America a more welcoming place for your sons and daughters. I pledge to you that if we are elected, you will have a friend and advocate in the White House.

—REPUBLICAN NATIONAL CONVENTION SPEECH IN
MINNEAPOLIS, SEPTEMBER 3, 2008

It was such an answered prayer the moment that Trig was born. It was the greatest, most obvious manifestation of a prayer . . . He looked up at me like he was saying, "I'm here[,] mom. Now are you going to trust that all is going to be OK?"

—ASSOCIATED PRESS, JULY 1, 2010

Q: McCain likes to get up early in the morning and go. And you?

A: Morning person. Yup. We don't sleep much. Too much to do. What I've had to do, though, is in the middle of the night, put down the Black[B]erry and pick up the breast pump. Do a couple of things different and still get it all done.

Q: As a new mom, how are you going to juggle all this?

A: I am thankful to be married to a man who loves being a dad as much as I love being a mom, so he is my strength. And practically speaking, we have a great network of help with lots of grandparents and aunties and uncles all around us. We have a lot of help.

Q: So will your husband be on leave now indefinitely to be Mr. Mom?

A: I would say so, yes.

—Sandra Sobieraj Westfall in *People* magazine, August 29, 2008

My heart is in this cause, making our country and hopefully ultimately our world a more welcoming place for those with special needs. What we're learning, certainly with our son, is that they teach us more than what we'll ever be able to teach them in these wonderful lessons. It's a blessed position that we're in.

—Before speaking about special-needs children at an upcoming fund-raiser, *Atlanta Journal-Constitution*, June 18, 2010

We're proud of Bristol's decision to have her baby and even prouder to become grandparents . . . Bristol and the young man she will marry are going to realize very quickly the difficulties of raising a child, which is why they will have the love and support of our entire family.

—AL JAZEERA ENGLISH, SEPTEMBER 3, 2008

Q: Governor Palin, when you were 13 weeks pregnant, last December, you had an amniocentesis that determined Trig had Down syndrome.

A: I was grateful to have all those months to prepare. I can't imagine the moms that are surprised at the end. I think they have it a lot harder.

—SANDRA SOBIERAJ WESTFALL IN *PEOPLE* MAGAZINE, AUGUST 29, 2008

I would like to see him apologize to young women across the country . . . for contributing to a culture . . . that says it's OK to talk about statutory rape . . . It's not cool; it's not funny . . . I don't find it humorous.

—COMMENTING ON *LATE NIGHT* HOST DAVID LETTERMAN'S JOKE ABOUT HER DAUGHTERS. DURING HIS OPENING MONOLOGUE, LETTERMAN SAID OF PALIN'S VISIT WITH HER FAMILY TO A NEW YORK YANKEES GAME, "THERE WAS ONE AWKWARD MOMENT DURING THE SEVENTH INNING STRETCH. HER DAUGHTER WAS KNOCKED UP BY ALEX RODRIGUEZ," *TODAY SHOW*, JUNE 12, 2009

Choosing life was the right road, the right choice. . . . It hasn't been easy, and society, culture sure hasn't been easy on her. Wow, our culture and our media has made it rough on her.

—On Bristol's pregnancy, which was announced days after Palin was named the vice-presidential nominee, Associated Press, May 14, 2010

I told a bad joke. I told a joke that was beyond flawed, and my intent is completely meaningless compared to the perception . . . It's not your fault that it was misunderstood—it's my fault. So I would like to apologize, especially to the two daughters involved, Bristol and Willow, and also to the governor and her family and everybody else who was outraged by the joke. I'm sorry about it, and I'll try to do better in the future. Thank you very much.

—David Letterman on his inappropriate joke about Bristol's pregnancy, Europe Intelligence Wire, June 16, 2009

Because I have both boys and girls I have a greater respect for equality and making sure that gender is not an issue and that everyone is treated equally.

—Time, August 14, 2008

It's not the most ideal situation, certainly you make the most of it . . . Bristol is a strong and bold woman, and she is an amazing mom. And this little baby is very lucky to have her as a mama. He's going to be just fine.

—ON DAUGHTER BRISTOL'S PREGNANCY, CNNPOLITICS.COM, FEBRUARY 17, 2009

"I was scared," Palin said, adding that she asked her husband, Todd, "Why us?" He responded, "Why not?"

"My family life is much richer thanks to this beautiful baby boy Trig. He is awesome."

—*MILWAUKEE JOURNAL SENTINEL*, NOVEMBER 6, 2009

My son being in a striker brigade in the army has really opened my eyes to international events, and how war impacts everyday Americans like us when we have a child who chooses to enlist and to serve [for] the right reasons. Certainly a child born with Down Syndrome has opened my eyes, too, to challenges that others have. Every American has a challenge. Every American has battles and bumps in the road in their lives. It's just really opened my eyes to a larger world than maybe what I had been used to.

—*TIME*, AUGUST 14, 2008

That's why I was shocked. Truthfully, we were devastated.

—On not knowing that their teenage daughter had been having sex with her boyfriend, UPI NewsTrack, November 14, 2009

This is what I've been telling Bristol, before she gets married, is, "Bristol, there are definitely gonna be tough parts in marriage. You have to look at those tough times and remember that you have essentially a business contract with this person. You've signed an agreement. You're going to be together. And you look at it that way as you work through the tough times, because I guarantee the better time is there on the other side." That's how we've looked at it.

—*Esquire*, March 2009

I don't know if the task [her son Track serving in Iraq] is from God . . . What I know is that my son has made a decision. I am so proud of his independent and strong decision he has made, what he decided to do and serving for the right reasons and serving something greater than himself and not choosing a real easy path where he could be more comfortable and certainly safer.

—AMERICA'S INTELLIGENCE WIRE, SEPTEMBER 11, 2008

You know, I looked at her [daughter Bristol] and I thought, *Bristol, honey, you're going to have to grow up really fast.* And she is a strong and kind-hearted young woman. She's going to make a great mom. And she is very strong. She's going to be just fine.

But Bristol has an opportunity, at this point, also, to reach out to other young American women and let them know that these are absolutely less-than-ideal circumstances that she or any other unwed teenage mother are [sic] in. And it is not something to glamorize. It's not something to condone, if you will. Bristol has an opportunity to reach out to other young mothers and help them and, hopefully, not see such a prevalence, also, of unwed teenage mothers. The rates are too high.

—*LARRY KING LIVE*, NOVEMBER 12, 2008

He [husband Todd] can go on just an hour or two of sleep a night. He says, "I can sleep when I die." There is no way I could have done this job without his tremendous contributions to the home life. He's able to keep it organized, like a well-oiled machine.

—*ANCHORAGE DAILY NEWS*, MAY 27, 2007

No woman should have to choose between her career, education and her child.

—*ANCHORAGE DAILY NEWS*, AUGUST 6, 2006

The toughest thing has been the shots taken against the kids, against the family. They're my kids. The mama grizzly bear in me comes out, makes me want to rear up on my hind legs and say, "Wait a minute." It's a little bit unfair there. It has nothing to do with taking the country in a new direction.

—*NEW YORK TIMES*, OCTOBER 20, 2008

My kids are cool, too! They are very adaptable. They have been used to all these years me having a very busy schedule as a oil and gas regulator and a city manager and mayor and then governor and then Todd being very busy with a commercial fishing schedule and North Slope oil production schedule . . . [I]t's a great, fun family that we have . . . And they, too, I believe have felt that this has been the privilege of a lifetime to be able to get to know John McCain, be able to run with him, with his family, with the team that we had together. They got to travel the country and see things that of course never would they have had an opportunity before, so it's been nothing but awesome.

—INTERVIEW WITH CNN'S WOLF BLITZER, NOVEMBER 12, 2008

Now as Governor I've been able to secure more assistance in funding for students with special needs, but as Vice President [I'll] be able to do so much more there making sure that these children and their families, that all of our families in America know family comes first; you'll have a friend and an advocate in the White House.

—SOUTHEAST MISSOURIAN, OCTOBER 30, 2008

ON FOREIGN POLICY

Alaskans are frustrated because there is opposition in Congress to developing our vast amount of natural resources. We want to contribute more to the rest of the United States. We want to help secure the United States, and help us get off this reliance of foreign sources of energy. It's a very nonsensical position we're in right now. We send President Bush and Secretary [of Energy Samuel] Bodman overseas to ask the Saudis to ramp up production of crude oil so that hungry markets in America can be fed, your sister state in Alaska has those resources. But these lands are locked up by Congress, and we are not allowed to drill to the degree America needs the development.

—*Investor's Business Daily*, July 11, 2008

Q: Have you ever met a foreign head of state?

A: I have not, and I think if you go back in history and if you ask that question of many vice presidents, they may have the same answer that I just gave you. But, again, we've got to remember what the desire is in this nation at this time. It is for no more politics as usual and somebody's big, fat résumé maybe that shows decades and decades in that Washington establishment, where, yes, they've had opportunities to meet heads of state.

—2008 ELECTION INTERVIEW WITH CHARLIE GIBSON, SEPTEMBER 11, 2008

Baroness Thatcher's life and career serve as a blueprint for overcoming the odds and challenging the "status quo." She started life as a grocer's daughter from Grantham and rose to become Prime Minister—all by her own merit and hard work. I cherish her example and will always count her as one of my role models. Her friendship with my other political hero, Ronald Reagan, exemplified the Special Relationship between the United States and the United Kingdom.

—WRITING ABOUT BRITISH PRIME MINISTER MARGARET THATCHER ON HER FACEBOOK PAGE, CITED BY CNN.COM, JUNE 15, 2010

Alaskans have been first-rate at international trade for decades. To our friends in international markets, thank you for your friendship and trade. Alaska welcomes your business and investment.

International trade is important to Alaska. Our exports grew more than 12 percent last year, and, for the first time, our annual exports topped $4 billion in 2006. We are helping our economy and economies around the world through trade.

In all our efforts, we will keep Alaska residents first. We will help Alaska businesses succeed in their key international markets. We will improve Alaska's positive international relations with our key trading partners. We will help open new doors.

—LETTER FROM THE GOVERNOR ON STATE TRADE ON THE ALASKA STATE WEB SITE WWW.ALASKA.GOV, SEPTEMBER 1, 2008

I disagree with the Obama administration on that. I believe that the Jewish settlements [in Israel] should be allowed to be expanded upon, because the population of Israel is going to grow. More and more Jewish people will be flocking to Israel in the days and weeks and months ahead. And I don't think that the Obama administration has any right to tell Israel that the Jewish settlements cannot expand.

—ABC NEWS, NOVEMBER 17, 2009

Q: Should the U.S. negotiate with leaders like President Assad [of the Syrian Arab Republic] and [President of the Islamic Republic of Iran] Ahmadinejad?

A: I think, with Ahmadinejad, personally, he is not one to negotiate with. You can't just sit down with him with no preconditions being met. Barack Obama is so off-base in his proclamation that he would meet with some of these leaders around our world who would seek to destroy America and that, and without preconditions being met. That's beyond naive. And it's beyond bad judgment. I've never heard Henry Kissinger say, "Yeah, I'll meet with these leaders without preconditions being met." Diplomacy is about doing a lot of background work first and shoring up allies and positions and figuring out what sanctions perhaps could be implemented if things weren't gonna go right. That's part of diplomacy.

—Interview with CBS's Katie Couric, September 24, 2008

I wanted to meet you for many years. The only flag at my office is an Israeli flag, and I want you to know and I want Israelis to know that I am a friend.

—On meeting President Shimon Peres of Israel, *New York Sun*, September 26, 2008

John McCain and I are committed to drawing attention to the danger posed by Iran's nuclear program, and we will not waver in our commitment. I will continue to call for sustained action to prevent Iranian President Ahmadinejad from getting these weapons that he wants for a second Holocaust.

—UNITED PRESS INTERNATIONAL, SEPTEMBER 19, 2008

I see the people around the globe, based on what we're hearing from leaders of other countries, they are looking at us in vain for our leadership. Some leaders are vacillating and even alienating our allies . . . This isn't a time when we want to poke an ally like Israel in the eye. We want to make sure that our allies know we are safe and secure and we will share our security with them.

—*PEORIA JOURNAL*, APRIL 19, 2010

What I think is that smaller democratic countries that are invaded by a larger power is something for us to be vigilant against . . . We have got to show the support, in this case, for [the Democratic Republic of] Georgia.

—AMERICA'S INTELLIGENCE WIRE, SEPTEMBER 12, 2008

ON GUN CONTROL

*Don't doubt for a minute that, if they [gun control advocates]
thought they could get away with it, they would ban guns and
ban ammunition and gut the Second Amendment. It's the job of
all of us at the NRA and its allies to stop them in their tracks.*

—To National Rifle Association members during their annual
meeting, as reported in the *Guardian* (U.K.), May 15, 2010

*This decision is a victory for all Alaskans and individual Americans.
The right to own guns and use them responsibly is something I and
many other Alaskans cherish. I applaud the Court for standing up for
the Constitution and the right of Americans to keep and bear arms.*

—Lauding the U.S. Supreme Court's decision upholding the right of
Americans to own guns for self-defense, hunting, and other purposes by
striking down Washington DC's 32-year-old ban on handguns, Alaska
Governor's Office: press release, *2nd Amendment*, June 26, 2008

I am a lifetime member of the NRA. I support our Constitutional right to bear arms and am a proponent of gun safety programs for Alaska's youth.

—CAMPAIGN WEB SITE, WWW.PALINFORGOVERNOR.COM, *ISSUES*, NOVEMBER 7, 2006

Left-wing groups talk about eating organic, wholesome food. We do that. We just happen to shoot it first . . . I have bad news for those groups. Bambi's mother is dinner—even in L.A. Where do those people think their venison comes from? The deer didn't die of natural causes. It wasn't road kill.

—*CHARLOTTE OBSERVER*, MAY 14, 2010

I want to fill my freezer with good, clean, healthy protein for my kids. That's what I was raised on. It is abundant, and it is available here in Alaska, with caribou and moose and different game and lots of very, very healthy and delicious wild Alaskan seafood. That's what we eat. So that's why I hunt and why I fish.

—*ESQUIRE*, MARCH 2009

ON HEALTH CARE

We used to hustle over the border for health care we received
in Canada. And I think now, isn't that ironic?

—*Huffington Post*, March 8, 2010

The America I know and love is not one in which my parents or my baby with Down Syndrome will have to stand
in front of Obama's "death panel" so his bureaucrats can
decide, based on a subjective judgment of their "level
of productivity in society," whether they are worthy of
health care. Such a system is downright evil.

—Posted on Facebook, August 7, 2009

I sure wish that the present tool being used to reform health care would die, but I don't trust as far as I can throw them some of the people who are saying, "Ok, we'll slow down." What they're working on today there in Congress and the White House, it needs to die.

—Fox News, February 7, 2010

I support flexibility in government regulations that allow competition in health care that is needed, and is proven to be good for the consumer, which will drive down health care costs and reduce the need for government subsidies. I also support patients in their rightful demands to have access to full medical billing information.

—Campaign Web site, www.palinforgovernor.com, *Issues*, November 7, 2006

ON THE WAR IN IRAQ

Q: Are we continuing on the proper course in Iraq?

A: In the past five years, there hasn't been a successful terrorist strike on United States soil, and that's no accident. It is our gratitude that we need to show to our military, to our troops for keeping us safe. I support them being over there. I support our president. I support our military. But of course, I want to see that exit strategy being developed and being revealed to our public. This hits me near and dear to my heart as I'm raising teenagers. A 17-year-old son who is interested in the military. Of course, you know I think about it every day, if that were my son or my daughter over there. I want our troops to come home safely.

> —Alaska 2006 governor debate, moderated
> by John Tracy, October 30, 2006

Pray for our military men and women who are striving to do what is right. Also, for this country, that our leaders, our national leaders, are sending soldiers out on a task that is from God. That's what we have to make sure that we're praying for, that there is a plan and that that plan is God's plan.

—TO STUDENTS AT THE WASILLA ASSEMBLY OF GOD, JUNE 2008

I have faith that all is going to be well. And my son, he's good. He is serving for the right reasons. He's a teenage kid who recognized that he had an opportunity to do all that he could, at his stage in life, to help protect America and to serve something greater than self. And I think about my son, I think about Track, in those terms and I think, is every elected official who is serving in government doing the same thing to the best of their ability? Are they protecting this country? Are they doing all that they can to make sure that our troops, over there especially, are well equipped, have the budget that they need, have all the tools that they need for them to do their jobs?

—CNN, NOVEMBER 12, 2008

I've been so focused on state government, I haven't really focused much on the war in Iraq. I heard on the news about the new deployments, and while I support our president [George W. Bush], Condoleezza Rice and the administration, I want to know that we have an exit plan in place; I want assurances that we are doing all we can to keep our troops safe. Every life lost is such a tragedy.

—Alaska Business Monthly, December 4, 2006

I have a 19-year-old who's getting ready to be deployed to Iraq. His striker brigade leaves on September 11 of this year. He's 19, and he'll be gone for a year. [And so] on a personal level, when I talk about the plan for the war, let's make sure we have a plan here.

—Time, August 14, 2008

We do have a plan for withdrawal. We don't need . . . early withdrawal out of Iraq. We cannot afford to lose there, or we're going to be no better off in the war in Afghanistan, either. We have got to win in Iraq, and with the surge that has worked . . . We cannot afford to lose against al-Qaida and the [Shiite] extremists who are still there, still fighting us, but we're getting closer and closer to victory and it would be a travesty if we quit now in Iraq.

—United Press International, October 2, 2008

ON IMMIGRATION REFORM

There is no ability or opportunity in there [Arizona law] for the racial profiling. Shame on the lame stream media again for turning this into something that it is not . . . It's shameful, too, that the Obama administration has allowed . . . this to become more of a racial issue by perpetuating this myth that racial profiling is a part of this law . . . I think that President Obama is playing to his base on this one. And I think that's quite unfortunate because this isn't fair to the legal immigrants. It's not fair to illegal immigrants either . . . many of them want to come here and find that pathway to citizenship.

—Politico.com, April 4, 2010

Q: Should undocumented immigrants be deported?

A: There is no way that in the U.S. we would round up every illegal immigrant. There are about 12 million of the illegal immigrants. It's just an impossibility, but that's not a humane way anyway to deal with the issue.

Q: Do you then favor an amnesty for the 12 million undocumented immigrants?

A: No, I do not. Not total amnesty. You know, people have got to follow the rules. We have got to make sure that there is equal opportunity. Those who are here legally should be first in line for services being provided and those opportunities that this great country provides.

Q: So you support a path to citizenship for undocumented immigrants?

A: I do, because I understand why people would want to be in America. To seek the safety and prosperity, the opportunities, the health that is here. It is so important that . . . people follow the rules so that people can be treated equally and fairly in this country.

—UNIVISION INTERVIEW BY JORGE RAMOS, OCTOBER 26, 2008

It's time for Americans across this great country to stand up and say, "We're all Arizonans now." And in clear unison we say, "Mr. President: Do your job. Secure our border."

—ASSOCIATED PRESS, MAY 17, 2010

Keeping the girls' basketball team off the court for political reasons? Those are fighting words. That's how they treat women in China.

—On a decision by a Chicago high school to cancel the girls basketball team's trip to a tournament in Arizona as a protest of the state's controversial immigration law, United Press International, May 13, 2010

The situation is that we have unsecure borders. Does this boycott of Arizona, an economic and political boycott of the people of Arizona, which will help no one—and in fact, it will hurt the Hispanic community within Arizona and everybody else—does it help secure the borders? No. Does it lead towards the immigration reform that needs to take place? Absolutely not. This just divides people. And I think that that is what some people are intending to do with this issue, just divide, make it kind of a partisan issue. And it's not partisan. Secure the borders!

—On the Record with Greta Van Susteren, May 14, 2010

ON JOHN MCCAIN

In politics, there are some candidates who use change to promote their careers. And then there are those, like John McCain, who use their careers to promote change.

—Republican National Convention speech in Minneapolis, September 3, 2008

With their usual certitude, they told us that all was lost—there was no hope for this candidate who said that he would rather lose an election than see his country lose a war. But the pollsters and pundits overlooked just one thing when they wrote him off. They overlooked the caliber of the man himself—the determination, resolve, and sheer guts of Senator John McCain. The voters knew better.

—Republican National Convention speech in Minneapolis, September 3, 2008

It was John McCain who refused to break faith with our
troops, who have now brought victory in Iraq right within
sight. As the mother of one of those troops, that is exactly
the kind of man I want as commander-in-chief.

—BLOOMBERG, SEPTEMBER 15, 2008

[We needed] more hours in the day so that we could have
reached more Americans with that message of who it is
that John McCain is. He is a true American hero; he does
have solutions in mind for this country to get the economy back on the right track and to win the wars. But he
now, as a leader in the Senate—we're going to be looking to
him, again, being able to unite the party, but also help to
unite the nation, working with the new administration.
John McCain has continued to be that strong leader in
America. And we need to listen to him.

—AFTER LOSING THE ELECTION, CNN, NOVEMBER 12, 2008

"Country First" is more than McCain's campaign slogan. That's going
to be printed on every page in the employee handbook if he's elected.

—*MISSOURIAN*, OCTOBER 30, 2008

[Senator John McCain] is the only one talking about the wars
America is fighting, and he isn't afraid to use the word "victory."

—COLLEGIAN, UNIVERSITY OF RICHMOND, OCTOBER 13, 2008

A fellow prisoner of war, a man named Tom Moe of Lancaster, Ohio, recalls looking through a pinhole in his cell door as Lieutenant Commander John McCain was led down the hallway, by the guards, day after day . . . As the story is told, When McCain shuffled back from torturous interrogations, he would turn toward Moe's door and flash a grin and thumbs up as if to say, "We're going to pull through this." My fellow Americans, that is the kind of man America needs to see us through these next four years.

—REPUBLICAN NATIONAL CONVENTION SPEECH IN
MINNEAPOLIS, SEPTEMBER 3, 2008

I want a president who isn't afraid to use the word
victory when he talks about wars that America is
fighting. I want a president ready on day one.

—UPI NEWSTRACK, OCTOBER 22, 2008

*I'm very, very encouraged, as we all understand that John McCain
knows, more so than any other leader in our nation today, that
for national security reasons we must be an energy-independent
nation. We must start taking the steps to get there. That's why he has
embraced offshore drilling. That's why he has embraced the ideal of
the alternative fuels also. And I'll keep working on him with ANWR.*

—*Hannity & Colmes*, September 17, 2008

---

*You can trust John McCain and me to keep our promises, because
we're the only candidates in this race with track records of
reform. I've done it up in the state of Alaska by confronting
the good ole boy network and cleaning up corruption and
greed there, vetoing wasteful spending. John McCain . . . he's
known in the U.S. Senate not just as the patriot but as the
maverick—he's taken on the wasteful spending and the abuse.*

—*Southeast Missourian*, October 30, 2008

ON THE MEDIA

If [the media] convince enough voters that that is negative campaigning for me to call Barack Obama out on his associations, then I don't know what the future of our country would be in terms of First Amendment rights and our ability to ask questions without fear of attacks by the mainstream media.

—WMAL-AM (Washington DC), October 31, 2008

I am thrilled to be joining the great talent and management team at Fox News. It's wonderful to be part of a place that so values fair and balanced news.

—Houston Chronicle, January 12, 2010

I am glad to be here on the president's home turf.
Somebody told me, "You know you're going into enemy
territory." I said, "It's Chicago—it's not MSNBC."

—*Huffington Post*, May 5, 2010

It's amazing to me that in the mainstream media, the claim
is that, "Well, she [Elena Kagan] doesn't have a record
because she's never been a judge before. So there's nothing
really to pursue." There's no there there. There's nothing to
say about her, really. That's been the message, really, sent
from the mainstream media. So it'll take others to dig in
there, help educate the public on who she is, what her positions are, and what intentions are in terms of interpreting
the Constitution. And then that would help all of us make
our minds whether we want her as a justice or not.

—On President Obama's nomination of solicitor general Elena
Kagan to replace retiring justice John Paul Stevens on the Supreme
Court, *On the Record with Great Van Susteren*, May 14, 2010

Sometimes you've got to trust your instincts, and when you don't
you end up in a place like this [the annual Gridiron Dinner]. . . . It
is good to be here though, really, in front of this audience of leading
journalists and intellectuals or, as I like to call it, "a death panel."

—*Christian Science Monitor*, December 6, 2009

Oprah, you're the queen. You have nothing to worry about.

—PALIN'S RESPONSE WHEN OPRAH WINFREY ASKED HER ABOUT THE POSSIBILITY OF
HAVING HER OWN TALK SHOW, *THE OPRAH WINFREY SHOW*, NOVEMBER 16, 2009

I think that the mainstream media is quite broken. And I think that there needs to be the fairness, the balance in there. That's why I'm doing Fox . . . As long as there is not the opinion under the guise of hard news story, I think that there needs to be clear differentiation . . . Well, I certainly don't ask for it [controversy]. Like so many other Americans with some strong convictions, some strong ideas, some solutions that I want to see meet the challenges in our country, I want to talk about them. I'm not one to want to sit down and shut up.

—ON THE ANNOUNCEMENT THAT SHE WOULD BECOME A FOX
NEWS CONTRIBUTOR, *TONIGHT SHOW*, MARCH 3, 2010

Yesterday the Anchorage Daily News, they called again to ask— double, triple, quadruple check—who is Trig's real mom? And I said, Come on, are you kidding me? We're gonna answer this? Do you not believe me or my doctor? And they said, No, it's been quite cryptic the way that my son's birth has been discussed. And I thought, Okay, more indication of continued problems in the world of journalism.

—*ESQUIRE*, MARCH 2009

In an attempt to "go incognito," I Sharpied the [John McCain]
logo out on my sun visor so photographers would be less likely
to recognize me and bother my kids or other vacationers . . .
I am so sorry if people took this silly incident the wrong way.
I adore John McCain, support him 100 percent and will do
everything I can to support his re-election . . . Todd and I have
since cut our vacation short because the incognito attempts
didn't work, and fellow vacationers were bothered for the two
days we spent in the sun. So much for trying to go incognito.

—AMERICA'S INTELLIGENCE WIRE, DECEMBER 18, 2010

I should have done it [the interview with Katie Couric],
yes. And her questions were fair. Obviously, being a bit
annoyed with some of the questions, my annoyance shows
through. And I am who I am, though, and I call it like I see
it. And some of those questions, you know, regarding what
I read up in Alaska, were, to me, a bit irrelevant . . . And to
attribute, I think, that interview to any kind of negativity
in the campaign or a downfall in the campaign, I think
it's ridiculous. And I wish that there . . . would have been,
perhaps, more dilution, in terms of that interview being
one of many, many. I wish I could have done more inter-
views along the trail.

—COMMENTING ON HER INTERVIEW WITH KATIE COURIC,
LARRY KING LIVE, NOVEMBER 12, 2008

Regarding information about my record that is now out there: Much of it that was based on misinformation. It was a very, very frustrating thing to have to go through when the record was never corrected. And we would try to correct the record, and too many in the media chose not to make those corrections.

What misinformation [in the media] are you talking about?

Some of the goofy things like who was Trig's mom. Well, I'm Trig's mom [raises her hand] and do you want to see my medical records to prove that? . . . And banning books. That was a ridiculous thing also that could have so easily been corrected just by a reporter taking an extra step and not basing a report on gossip or speculation. But just looking into the record. It was reported that I tried to ban Harry Potter when it hadn't even been written when I was the mayor. So, gosh, we have so many examples, I mean every day, especially the first few weeks, every day something that was thrown out there.

—*ANCHORAGE DAILY NEWS*, NOVEMBER 9, 2008

I've decided to stop in cities that are not usually
included in a typical book tour.

—ON DOING BOOK SIGNINGS IN GRAND RAPIDS, MICHIGAN; FORT
WAYNE, INDIANA; WASHINGTON, PENNSYLVANIA; AND ROANOKE,
VIRGINIA, UPI NEWSTRACK, NOVEMBER 16, 2009

GRETA VAN SUSTEREN: So women get a little different treatment, you think, overall in the media or not?
SARAH PALIN: Oh, man! Yes, they do! Not going to
whine about it or complain about it. It just makes
women, I think, work harder, produce better, be
more efficient . . . forcing us to articulate, I think,
our positions.

—*ON THE RECORD WITH GRETA VAN SUSTEREN*, MAY 14, 2010

A corrupt, deceptive, and manipulative media can ruin the
lives of good people, disrupt families, destroy reputations, and
ultimately hurt our country. Thank goodness for social networking
sites like this and new media sites which have allowed us to
get around the "lamestream" media and present the facts.

—PALIN'S FACEBOOK PAGE AS QUOTED BY CBSNEWS.COM, JUNE 1, 2010

BILL O'REILLY: Why did you boot it [the interview with Katie Couric]? I mean, if somebody asks what do you read? I say I read the *New York Times*, the *Wall Street Journal*, the *Washington Post*. I can reel them off in my sleep. You couldn't do it?

SARAH PALIN: Well, of course I could. Of course, I could.

BILL O'REILLY: Why didn't you?

SARAH PALIN: It's ridiculous to suggest that or to say that I couldn't tell people what I read, because by that point already it was relatively early in that multi-segmented interview with Katie Couric. It was quite obvious that it was going to be a bit of an annoying interview with the badgering of the questions. It seemed to me that she didn't know anything about Alaska, about my job as governor, about my accomplishments as a mayor or a governor, my record. And a question like that, though, yeah, I booted it. I screwed up. I should have been more patient and more gracious in my answer. It seemed to me that the question was more along the lines of, do you read? How do you stay in touch with the real world?

—*THE O'REILLY FACTOR*, NOVEMBER 19, 2009

If there's any connection there to President Obama taking so doggone long to get in there, to dive in there, and grasp the complexity and the potential tragedy that we are seeing here in the Gulf of Mexico—now, if this was President Bush or if this were a Republican in office . . . you know the mainstream media would be all over his case in terms of asking questions why the administration didn't get in there and make sure that the regulatory agencies were doing what they were doing with the oversight to make sure that things like this don't happen.

—ST. PETERSBURG TIMES, MAY 24, 2010

ON POLITICIANS

What's happening to politicians, especially in Washington, is they're becoming addicted to "opium," O.P.M.: other people's money.

—MINNESOTA DAILY, APRIL 4, 2010

I might add that in small towns, we don't quite know what to make of a candidate [Barack Obama] who lavishes praise on working people when they are listening, and then talks about how bitterly they cling to their religion and guns when those people aren't listening. We tend to prefer candidates who don't talk about us one way in Scranton and another way in San Francisco.

—REPUBLICAN NATIONAL CONVENTION SPEECH IN MINNEAPOLIS, SEPTEMBER 3, 2008

Politics isn't just a game of competing interests and clashing parties. The people of America expect us to seek public office and to serve for the right reasons. And the right reason is to challenge the status quo and to serve the common good.

—SPEECH DELIVERED IN DAYTON, OHIO ON AUGUST 29, 2008

Q: Explain how you took on your own party as governor of Alaska. And do you think you'd be able to do that, as well, in Washington?

A: Well, I just recognized that it doesn't matter which party it is. It's just kind of creating the good-old-boy network and the cronyism and allowing obsessive partisanship to get in the way of just doing what's right for the people who are to be served . . . Sometimes it's our own party that just starts taking advantage of the people. And I felt compelled to do something about it, decided to run for office, got in there and with that mandate that I believe the people had just given me, via their vote, they expected the changes to take place, that reform. And we're living up to that. And as we do, we are ruffling feathers.

—FOX NEWS, SEPTEMBER 17, 2008

GLENN BECK: Who's your favorite Founder?

PALIN: You know, well, because they came collectively together with so much diversity in terms of belief but collectively they came together to form this Union.

BECK: [Bull]. Who's your favorite?

PALIN: George Washington, because he returned power to the people and then returned to Mount Vernon to farm. They were led by, of course, George Washington. So he's got to rise to the top. Washington was the consummate statesman. He served; he turned power to the people. He didn't want to be a king. He returned power to the people. Then he went back to Mount Vernon. He went back to his farm. He was almost reluctant to serve as president too, and that's who you need to find to serve in government, in a bureaucracy—those who you know will serve for the right reasons because they're reluctant to get out there and seek a limelight and seek power. They're doing it for the people; that was George Washington.

—*The Glenn Beck Show*, January 13, 2010

—————

I think that every politician who wants to run for office should have run a business before.

—Speaking at the International Council of Shopping Centers meeting, as reported by UPI.com, May 24, 2010

[Ron Paul's] cool. He's a good guy. He's so independent. He's independent of the party machine, and I'm like, "Right on!" you know, so am I . . . Americans are tiring of the obsessed partisanship that gets in the way of just doing the right thing for this country.

—COMMENTING ON RON PAUL, THE TEXAS CONGRESSMAN WHO
WAS A 2008 CANDIDATE FOR THE REPUBLICAN NOMINATION
FOR PRESIDENT, MTV, FEBRUARY 5, 2008

And if they don't want to disclose what they do, I think they need to make a choice. Are they going to be a law-maker, serving Alaskans, or are they going to serve the company that's paying them? . . . If a legislator is working just a few hours for thousands of dollars, that smells to the public like a bribe.

—ON A BILL THAT WOULD HAVE REQUIRED LAWMAKERS TO REVEAL MORE
ABOUT HOW THEY GET THEIR MONEY. THE BILL FAILED TO REACH A VOTE
IN THE LEGISLATURE, *ANCHORAGE DAILY NEWS*, SEPTEMBER 9, 2006

The advantages of being an outsider, if you will, far outweigh the disadvantages.

—REFERRING TO HER APPOINTMENT OF TALIS COLBERG AS ALASKA ATTORNEY
GENERAL, *KNIGHT-RIDDER/TRIBUNE BUSINESS NEWS*, DECEMBER, 14, 2006

ON POLITICS

Well, it's always, though, safer in politics to avoid risk. To just go along with the status quo. But I didn't get into government to do the safe and easy things. A ship in harbor is safe, but that's not why the ship is built. Politics isn't just a game of competing interests and clashing parties. The people of America expect us to seek public office and to serve for the right reasons. And the right reason is to challenge the status quo and to serve the common good.

—Speech in Dayton, Ohio, covered by NPR, August 29, 2008

Nobody should ever be afraid of these contested primaries. Competition is good. This is democracy at work.

—Speaking at a fund-raiser for the state of Arkansas Republican Party, *Arkansas News*, February 16, 2010

I used to wonder if the occasionally rough edges of politics
were unique here under the Great North Star. But I ventured
out a bit this past year, and I tell you that, as partisan
quarrels go, ours [in Alaska] really aren't so bad.

—ALASKA DISPATCH, JANUARY 22, 2009

CNN: If you guys [McCain and Palin] win, you'll both most likely be working with a Democratic Congress. It's gonna be a slow process. What I'm trying to find out from you—from John McCain as well—day one, people want a difference, to make a difference in the economy, as we're seeing daily swings in the stock market, houses going foreclosed on . . .

SARAH PALIN: Well, day one, you bring in everyone around that table, too, you bring in the congressional leadership, and, assuming that there will be, certainly, Democrats, at that table, that's good, too; these are gonna be bipartisan approaches that must be taken, I have that executive experience also having formed a cabinet up there in Alaska that, you know, we've got independents and Democrats and Republicans whom I have appointed to our administrative positions. We have the best of ideas coming together in order to best serve the people.

John McCain, too, he's been known as the maverick to take on his own party when need be, to reach over the aisle and work with the other party also. Now, Barack Obama has not been able to do that; he's gone with—what is it?—96 percent of the time with Democrat leadership? Not having that, I think, ability or willingness to work with the other side. So as an executive, we need to create a team that is full of good ideas and not let obsessive partisanship get in the way, as we start taking measures to shore up our economy, which already Congress is working on with the rescue package, with some of the bailout packages, the provisions in there that can work, too, but it's gonna take everybody working together.

—INTERVIEW WITH CNN'S DREW GRIFFIN, OCTOBER 21, 2008

I will go around the country on behalf of candidates who believe in the right things, regardless of their party label or affiliation. People are so tired of the partisan stuff. Even my own son is not a Republican.

—WASHINGTON (DC) TIMES, JULY 12, 2009

RUNNER'S WORLD: What has running taught you about politics?

SARAH PALIN: Same thing it's taught me about life: You have to have determination and set goals, and you don't complain when something's hurting because no one wants to hear it. You get bummed and burned out sometimes in running and in politics, but if you're in for the long haul and you're in it because you know that it is a good thing, then you get out there and you do it anyway. You know, [former *Runner's World* columnist] George Sheehan really could articulate what running means in terms of applicability to life. During the campaign, when people asked me about my favorite authors, I said C. S. Lewis, John Steinbeck, and Dr. George Sheehan, and people would look at me, these reporters are like, "Who in the world is that?" But his books and columns so inspired me 10, 15, 20 years ago, and still do. I remember what he wrote about applying the lessons of running to relationships and families and businesses and, in my case, running a state. He was a brilliant man.

—*Runner's World*, August 2009

ON THE RECESSION

Q: Who is to blame for the subprime lending meltdown?

A: It was predator lenders who tried to talk Americans into thinking that it was smart to buy a $300,000 house if they could only afford a $100,000 house. There was deception, and there was greed and there was corruption. Joe Six Pack, hockey moms across the nation, we need to band together and say, "Never again." We need to demand from the federal government strict oversight of those entities in charge of our investments and our savings. Let's do what our parents told us before we probably even got that first credit card. Don't live outside of our means.

—VICE PRESIDENTIAL DEBATE AGAINST JOE BIDEN, OCTOBER 2, 2008

*The fact is that Fannie Mae and Freddie Mac have
gotten too big and too expensive to the taxpayers.*

—*Huffington Post, September 8, 2008*

Q: Was the [Bush Administration financial] bailout the worst of Washington or the best?

A: A good barometer is go to a kid's soccer game and turn to a parent and ask, "How are you feeling about the economy?" You're going to hear fear. Two years ago, it was John McCain who pushed so hard with the Fannie and Freddie reform measures. There will be greater oversight, thanks to John McCain's bipartisan efforts that he was so instrumental in bringing folks together, even suspending his own campaign to put politics aside.

—*Vice presidential debate against Joe Biden, October 2, 2008*

---

*Say what you will about the humble Eureka College–educated
Ronald Reagan, but he could have told our Harvard-educated
president that his debt-ridden exercise . . . will not play in Peoria.*

—*Peoria Journal, April 19, 2010*

Q: Senator Obama attacked Senator McCain for saying that the "fundamentals of the economy are strong." Are the fundamentals strong?

A: Well, it was an unfair attack on the verbiage that Senator McCain chose to use, because the fundamentals, as he explained afterwards, he means our workforce; he means the ingenuity of the American. And of course, that is strong and that is the foundation of our economy. Certainly, the economy is a mess. And there have been abuses on Wall Street and that adversely affects Main Street. We've got to cure this.

Q: Through reform?

A: Through reform, absolutely. Look at the oversight that has been lax; it's a 1930s' type of regulatory regime overseeing some of these corporations. And we've got to get a more coordinated and a much more stringent oversight regime. Not that government is going to be solely looked to for the answers in all of the problems in Wall Street, but government can play a very, very appropriate role in the oversight.

—*HANNITY & COLMES*, SEPTEMBER 17, 2008

I didn't feel stimulated.

—ON THE PRESIDENT'S $787 BILLION FEDERAL STIMULUS PLAN, AS REPORTED IN *THE STATE* (SOUTH CAROLINA), MAY 15, 2010

Q: Who is responsible for these failing institutions [such as AIG and Lehman Bros., in the mortgage crisis], in your view?

A: I think the corruption on Wall Street—that is to blame. And that violation of the public trust. And that contract that should be inherent in corporations who are spending, investing other people's money—the abuse of that is what has got to stop. And it's a matter, too, of some of these CEOs and top management people and shareholders not holding that management accountable, being addicted to, we call it, O-P-M, "other people's money." Spending that, investing that, not using the prudence that we expect of them. But here again, government has got to play an appropriate role in the stringent oversight, making sure that those abuses stop.

—*HANNITY & COLMES*, SEPTEMBER 17, 2008

I would start cutting taxes and allowing our small businesses to keep more of what they are earning, more of what they are producing, more of what they own and earn so that they could start reinvesting in their businesses and expand and hire more people. Not punishing them by forcing health care reform down their throats; by not forcing an energy policy down their throats that ultimately will tax them more and cost them more to stay in business.

—INTERVIEW WITH BARBARA WALTERS, ABCNEWS.COM, NOVEMBER 17, 2009

Our country is at a crossroads. We have an out-of-touch
government in Washington. And the government wants to
tax and spend and borrow our way out of problems.

—WLTX-TV (Columbia, SC), May 14, 2010

Look at the oversight that has been lax, I believe, here it's a
1930s type of regulatory regime overseeing some of these
corporations. And we've got to get a more coordinated
and a much more stringent oversight regime. Not that
government is going to be solely looked to for the answers
in all of the problems in Wall Street, but government can
play a very, very appropriate role in the oversight as people are trusting these companies with their life savings,
with their investments, with their insurance policies and
construction bonds and everything else.

—Philly.com, September 18, 2008

We were told by this administration with this high
unemployment—now upwards of 10 percent—that that's the
new normal. Is that the new normal? . . . I think the new
normal will be when Speaker Pelosi loses her gavel, and the new
normal is when Harry Reid joins the unemployment line.

—Minnesota Public Radio, April 7, 2010

I'm ill about the position that America is in and that we have to look at a $700 billion bailout. At the same time we know that inaction is not an option, and as Senator McCain has said: unless this nearly trillion-dollar bailout is what it may end up to be, unless there are amendments in [Secretary of the Treasury Hank] Paulson's proposal, really I don't believe that Americans are going to support this, and we will not support this.

—*Financial Times* [U.K.] September 25, 2008

WOLF BLITZER: Right now a big issue: should the U.S. government, the federal government, bail out the big three automakers?

SARAH PALIN: Oh, that is the discussion of the day. And there is going to come a point here where absolutely the federal government must play an appropriate role in shoring up some of these industries that are hurting and will ultimately hurt our entire economy and the world's economy if there aren't some better decisions being made.

But we also have to start shifting some debate here in our country and start talking about personal responsibility and responsibility of management in some of these corporations and companies so that from henceforth it's not assumed that the federal government is going to be bailing out everybody who is going to soon line up, Wolf, for more taxpayer assistance.

—Interview with CNN's Wolf Blitzer, November 12, 2008

I am very happy to hear about that miniscule decrease there in the unemployment rate, but better that than a growing unemployment rate. The point is that we have lost millions and millions and millions of jobs as we have incurred greater and greater debt and deficit, debt that I believe is immoral because we're handing the bill to our children . . .

The point being, millions of jobs have been lost because, I think, Chris, what's coming from the White House is just a fundamental difference from a lot of conservatives in our belief that government is not the answer. The bailouts, the takeovers of the private sector—that's not the answer. That is not what built this great country into the most prosperous, healthiest, safest country on earth. No. It is free enterprise. It's the innovation, and work ethic of our small businesses, and our entrepreneurs. Empowering them to be able to keep more of what they earn, and reinvest according to their priorities. And then be able to create jobs—one—one job at a time with the principles that are free market—free enterprise based.

I don't think that is what we're seeing coming out of the White House.

—Interview with Fox News's Chris Wallace, February 7, 2010

As for the economic bailout provisions and the measures that have already been taken, it is a time of crisis and government *did* have to step in playing an appropriate role to shore up the housing market to make sure that we're thawing out some of the potentially frozen credit lines and credit markets; government did have to step in there. But now that we're hearing that the Democrats want an additional stimulus package or bailout package for what, hundreds of billions of dollars more? This is not a time to use the economic crisis as an excuse for reckless spending and for greater, bigger government and to move the private sector to the back burner and let government be assumed to be the be-all, end-all solution to the economic challenges that we have. That's what's scaring me now about hearing that the Democrats have an even greater economic bailout package, but we don't know all the details of it yet, and we'll certainly pay close attention to it.

—INTERVIEW WITH CNN'S DREW GRIFFIN, OCTOBER 21, 2008

I know what Americans are going through there. And you know, even today, Todd and I are looking at what's going on in the stock market, the relatively low number of investments that we have, looking at the hit that we're taking, probably $20,000 dollars last week in his 401(k) plan that was hit. I'm thinking, "Geez, the rest of America, they're facing the exact same thing that we are. We understand what the problems are."

—CNN, OCTOBER 1, 2008

How can we discuss reform without addressing the government policies at the root of the [economic] problems? The root of the collapse? And how can we think that setting up the Fed as the monitor of systemic risk in the financial sector will result in meaningful reform? The words *fox* and *henhouse* come to mind. The Fed's decisions helped create the bubble. Look at the root cause of most asset bubbles, and you'll see the Fed somewhere in the background . . . Lack of government wasn't the problem; government policies were the problem. The marketplace didn't fail. It became exactly as common sense would expect it to. The government ordered the loosening of lending standards. The Federal Reserve kept interest rates low. The government forced lending institutions to give loans to people who as I say, couldn't afford them. Speculators spotted new investment vehicles, jumped on board and rating agencies underestimated risks. So many to be blamed on so many different levels, but the fact remains that these people were responding to a market solution created by government policies that ran contrary to common sense.

—*Wall Street Journal*, September 23, 2009

ON FAITH

We hear of a judge's ruling that our National Day of Prayer is unconstitutional. I think we'll be challenging that one. God truly has shed his grace on thee—on this country. He's blessed us, and we better not blow it.

—ABCNEWS.COM, APRIL 20, 2010

This nation needs you. Know the facts. Stand for what's right. Don't be discouraged by the mocking of those who want to claim we just cling to our religion. I'm the first to admit—yeah, I do cling to my faith. That's all I've got.

—LOUISVILLE COURIER-JOURNAL, APRIL 16, 2010

---

*Somebody sent me the other day, Isaiah 49:16, and you need
to go home and look it up . . . [God] says, in that passage,
"I wrote your name on the palm of my hand to remember
you," and I'm like, "Okay, I'm in good company."*

—ON GETTING FLACK ABOUT WRITING NOTES ON HER HAND DURING
HER TEA PARTY CONVENTION SPEECH, MARCH 5, 2010

I can do my job there [in Alaska] in developing our natural resources and doing things like getting the roads paved and making sure our troopers have their cop cars and their uniforms and their guns, and making sure our public schools are funded. But really all of that stuff doesn't do any good if the people of Alaska's heart isn't right with God.

—SPEAKING AT THE WASILLA ASSEMBLY OF GOD, MINISTRY SCHOOL,
REPORTED IN THE *ANCHORAGE DAILY NEWS*, SEPTEMBER 4, 2008

*Faith is very, very important in my life. I don't believe I wear it
on my sleeve, and I would never try to shove it down anybody
else's throat and try to convert anybody. But just a very simple
faith that is important to me; it really is my foundation.*

—*HANNITY & COLMES*, SEPTEMBER 17, 2008

I do believe that there is purpose in everything. And for me personally I put my life in God's hands and ask Him to—don't let me miss some open door that He has for me, and I'll travel through that. I think the same thing for our nation as we seek God's guidance, His wisdom, His favor and protection over our nation, that at the end of the day, that the right thing is done. And I do believe that prayers were answered, others who prayed across this nation in the election that this nation would be protected, that we would be safe, that we would be prosperous and favored. I believe that prayer is answered.

—CNN, NOVEMBER 12, 2008

I would never presume to know God's will or to speak God's words.

—*RECORD* (BERGEN COUNTY, NJ), SEPTEMBER 12, 2008

Q: Are you offended by the phrase "under God" in the Pledge of Allegiance?

A: Not on your life. If it was good enough for the founding fathers, it's good enough for me and I'll fight in defense of our Pledge of Allegiance.

—EAGLE FORUM 2006 GUBERNATORIAL CANDIDATE QUESTIONNAIRE, JULY 31, 2006

ON THE GOP

A lot of Republican governors have really good ideas for our nation, because we're the ones there on the front lines being held accountable every single day in service to the people who have hired us in our own states; the planks in our platform are strong, and they are good for America. It's all about free enterprise.

—CNN, November 12, 2008

The Republicans have been getting criticized lately with this mistaken concept . . . sort of surrounding Republicans right now that they are the "party of no." And we are saying, what's wrong with being the "party of no," when you consider what it is that Obama, Pelosi, and Reid are trying to do to our country? So be it!

—Minnesota Public Radio, April 7, 2010

You're absolutely right on the cleansing that's needed
in our party—in the Republican Party.

—*KUDLOW & CO.*, AUGUST 1, 2008

I believe that Republicans in Washington have got to understand that the people of America are not fully satisfied with all the dealings within the party. Same applies though for the other party, also. Americans are just getting sick and tired of politics as usual, that embracing of the status quo, going with the flow and just assuming that the people of America are not noticing that we have opportunities for good change.

—*HANNITY & COLMES*, SEPTEMBER 17, 2008

The GOP needs to live the planks of its
platform, not just offer lip service.

—NEWSMAX.COM, AUGUST 29, 2008

[The Republicans] know best how to produce and contribute and grow and thrive and prioritize their income and what it is they produce. Those things that are part of the Republican [P]arty plank and platform, that's what Republicans need to get back to and not disappoint the electorate this go around.

—*Atlanta Journal Constitution*, June 18, 2010

ON RUNNING
FOR OFFICE

I'm like, "OK, God, if there is an open door for me
somewhere,"—this is what I always pray—" . . . don't let me
miss the open door. Show me where the open door is."

—On never saying never regarding running for political
office, Fox News interview, November 10, 2008

As for vice president, it would be certainly an exciting
thing to consider, but to me it's so farfetched and out
there that I don't spend any time thinking about it
because we have so many things to do in Alaska.

—Investor's Business Daily, July 11, 2008

Q: What got you involved in politics?

A: I studied journalism in college and always had an interest in the newsroom, which was of course so often focused on politics and government. But even earlier than that, my dad was an elementary school teacher, so often our dinner-table conversations were about current events and about those things that an elementary school teacher teaches students—much about government and much about our nation, and so I had ingrained in me an interest in our government, how things worked. And then from there I just became interested in more practical steps that I could take. I started off running for city council when I was very young in Wasilla, where I had grown up, and was elected to two terms on the city council. And then I realized to be really able to make a difference—not just being one of six of a body but to make a difference—I would have to run for the top-dog position, and so I ran for mayor and was elected mayor for two terms.

—Q&A WITH *TIME*'S JAY NEWTON SMALL, AUGUST 14, 2008

That was a little bit unexpected, how brutal some of that was.

—ON HOW DIFFICULT IT WAS TO READ WHAT WAS WRITTEN ABOUT HER CHILDREN, KNIGHT RIDDER WASHINGTON (DC) BUREAU, NOVEMBER 1, 2008

Keeping it simple is my philosophy. My desire is to see small, efficient government that's going to provide the basic services for Alaska, that's shared by the majority of Alaskans.

—ON RUNNING FOR GOVERNOR, *ANCHORAGE DAILY NEWS*, OCTOBER 26, 2005

DAVID BRODY: Let me ask you a little bit about some of these rallies. I know that some people [including] John McCain have called [some people] fringe [because of the derogatory] things said out there about Barack Obama at his rallies. Do you feel a responsibility when those are said to say, "Enough of this type of talk"?

SARAH PALIN: Absolutely. But what we have heard through some mainstream media is that folks have hollered out some pretty atrocious and unacceptable things, like "Kill him." If I ever were to hear that standing up there at the podium with the microphone, I would call 'em out on that, and I would tell these people, "No, that's unacceptable; let's rise above that, please." We haven't heard that. What I have heard, though is—even in the other camp, though—some negativity that has been injected in the campaign with the candidate himself, with Barack Obama telling his supporters to get out there and—I quote—"get in their face, argue with them." That's kind of inciting and a bit negative, and John McCain and I will have nothing to do with that.

—*THE BRODY FILE*, CBS NEWS, OCTOBER 20, 2008

If I were giving advice to myself back on the day my candidacy was announced, I'd say, "Tell the campaign that you'll be calling some of the shots." Don't just assume that they know you well enough to make all your decisions for you. Let them know that you're the CEO of a state, you're forty-four years old, and you've got a lot of great life experience that can be put to good use as a candidate.

—*Esquire*, March 2009

As for that VP talk all the time, I'll tell you, I still can't answer that question until somebody answers for me what is it exactly that the VP does every day? I'm used to being very productive and working real hard in an administration. We want to make sure that that VP slot would be a fruitful type of position.

—*Kudlow & Co.*, August 1, 2008

Being a mom, one very concerned about a son in the war, about a special needs child, about kids heading off to college—how are we going to pay those tuition bills? . . . We know what other Americans are going through as they sit around the kitchen table and try to figure out how are they going to pay out of pocket for health care. We've been there also, so that connection was important.

—On connecting with voters, America.gov, October 3, 2008

We've talked a lot about that [my role as vice president], John McCain and I have, about the missions that I'll get to embark on if we are so blessed to be hired by the American people to work for them. It's gonna be government reform, because that is what I've been able to do as a mayor and as a governor. You take on the special interests and the self-dealings. Yep, you ruffle feathers and you have the scars to prove it afterwards, but you have to take that on to give the American people that faith back in their own government. This is their government and we gotta put it back on their side. So, government reform and energy independence, can't wait to work on that . . . The other mission that John and I are anxious for me to lead on is helping our families who have children with special needs, ushering in that spirit to Washington, D.C., where we're gonna give every child a chance, and a good educational opportunity will be provided. That's gonna be a matter, too, of prioritizing the federal dollars that are already there and making sure that every child is given opportunity.

—INTERVIEW WITH CNN's DREW GRIFFIN, OCTOBER 21, 2008

In this election, it's a choice between a candidate who won't disavow a group committing voter fraud, and a leader who won't tolerate voter fraud.

—SPEAKING AT ELON UNIVERSITY, AS REPORTED IN THE *MEADVILLE* (PENNSYLVANIA) *TRIBUNE*, OCTOBER 16, 2008

It is not mean-spirited and it is not negative campaigning to call someone out on their plans and their record and their associations. It is not negative campaigning. It is in fairness to you, the voters, so we're going to call them out.

—*Roanoke Times*, October 28, 2008

You know I think that there is so much blame to go around, if you will, in terms of why it was that the Republican ticket did not win. We didn't get the Hispanic vote—that really hurt; we were outspent tremendously because, of course, Obama took the private financing; John McCain stuck to his promise of just keeping the public financing of the campaign, so was greatly outspent. Barack Obama was a great campaigner; he had a very strong organization. So many reasons; I'm not going to look backwards there again and point to just President Bush and the administration as to why our ticket didn't prevail.

—Interview with CNN's Wolf Blitzer, November 12, 2008

Our ticket [McCain/Palin] has the track record that proves we can do this. We haven't just been talking the talk. We've been walking the walk.

—*Missourian*, October 30, 2008

I did not order the clothes. Did not ask for the clothes. I would have been happy to have worn my own clothes from Day 1. But that is kind of an odd issue, an odd campaign issue as things were wrapping up there as to who ordered what and who demanded what.

—The Canadian Broadcasting Corporation (CBC), November 11, 2008

On November 4, we're going to set a course for the future of our great country. We're going to go one direction or the other, and you understand that our ticket, what we're all about is pro-growth, pro–private sector. We're tax cuts. We're reining in government. We're proponents of the culture of life that would make America better off. We're adamant about winning the wars with the strongest military in the world. All those things that we stand for that I think are so clearly articulated with our message, with the plan that's been expressed, we can go in that direction or we can go in the complete opposite direction of all those aforementioned goals that we have in mind if you choose the other ticket.

—*The Rush Limbaugh Show*, October 14, 2008

The truth is, though, I'm glad I'm not vice president. I'm glad because I would not know what to do with all that free time.

—*The Tonight Show*, March 2, 2010

The Flyers fans, they get so enthused that they boo everybody at the drop of a puck . . . OK, OK, I'm getting used to the boos already.

—On attending a Philadelphia Flyers hockey game after saying that she would be cheering for New York Rangers center Scott Gomez, who is from Anchorage, *Philadelphia Inquirer*, October 12, 2008

If I hurt the ticket at all and cost John McCain even one vote, I am sorry about it, because John McCain is a true American hero. He's got great solutions in terms of the challenges that are facing America right now, with national security and needing to get our economy back on the right track . . . I personally don't think that I, Sarah Palin from Alaska, the VP pick, I don't believe that I caused the outcome to be what it was. I think the economy tanking—tanking a couple of months ago—had a lot more to do with it than the VP pick . . . But again, you know, if I caused even one person to shy away from electing an American hero, John McCain, to the presidency, then I apologize.

—*Larry King Live*, November 12, 2008

We started this campaign talking about trust and transparency. And that's where we're ending it.

—*News & Observer* (Raleigh, NC), October 18, 2008

Not only am I ready but willing and able to serve as vice president with Senator McCain if Americans so bless us and privilege us with the opportunity of serving them. I'm ready with my executive experience as a city mayor and manager, as a governor, as a commissioner, a regulator of oil and gas.

—Answering criticism about her readiness for high office, *Houston Chronicle*, September 30, 2008

Long ago, a young farmer and haberdasher from Missouri followed an unlikely path to the vice presidency. A writer observed: "We grow good people in our small towns, with honesty, sincerity, and dignity." I know just the kind of people that writer had in mind when he praised Harry Truman.

—At the Republican National Convention, quoted by the *Kansas City Star*, September 22, 2008

The shots that perhaps our campaign has taken—it's nothing compared to the shots that some people across America are taking today. The things that really matter. Somebody worried about losing their house because of Wall Street collapses. Somebody worried about losing their job or being able to pay for their child's health care coverage or a parent perhaps having lost a son or daughter in battle. Those are the shots that matter. I'm going to keep it all in perspective.

—*Hannity & Colmes*, September 17, 2008

Q: Why do you think your campaign lost?

A: I think the Republican ticket represented too much of the status quo, too much of what had gone on in these last eight years, that Americans were kind of shaking their heads going, "[W]ait a minute, how did we run up a 10 trillion dollar debt in a Republican administration?" How have there been blunders with war strategy under a Republican administration? If we're talking change, we want to get far away from what it was that the present administration represented and that is to a great degree what the Republican Party at the time had been representing. So people desiring change I think went as far from the administration that is presently seated as they could. It's amazing that we did as well as we did.

—*ANCHORAGE DAILY NEWS*, NOVEMBER 9, 2008

The media strategy was a bit perplexing for at least those on the vice presidential side of the ticket, and not really understanding where we were going there with the relationships with the media. It was just an indication of maybe some things in our campaign being out of touch with the normal everyday average American who wanted to truly connect with the candidate.

—*THE O'REILLY FACTOR*, NOVEMBER 19, 2009

It's not on my radar screen right now.

—ASKED IF SHE WOULD RUN FOR NATIONAL OFFICE IN 2012, *THE OPRAH WINFREY SHOW*, NOVEMBER 15, 2009

———————

I would be willing to if I believe that it's right for the country.

—ON RUNNING FOR PRESIDENT IN 2012, FOXNEWS.COM, FEBRUARY 7, 2010

ON TAXES

Let me bring up one more thing real quickly about the economy and taxes and Barack Obama and his flip-flopping and his inconsistencies . . . This stuff should make people question what his intentions are. Now, we're pressing Obama on taxes, right, because he's known as somebody who would raise taxes on you. He's voted 94 times for higher taxes, including increased taxes on people making just $42,000 a year. So, he said repeatedly he would consider abandoning his plan for all these huge tax increases of his if the economy was—quote—"weak." He said if it were weak. But even today, not being able to admit that, okay, the economy is weak, but it's not weak enough for Obama to say he won't raise taxes. He will raise taxes. People have to understand that and then, from there, let them make the best decision.

—*The Rush Limbaugh Show*, October 14, 2008

I guess I don't have enough grace to apply to Jerry Brown when he says he isn't going to be one for taxing Americans. Look what he did when he was governor. Look at what the foundation has been built upon there in California and he had been a part of that and that was spending outside of their means. I guess I don't have enough grace to say[,] "Hey Jerry, I believe ya."

—*SACRAMENTO BEE*, JUNE 9, 2010

Q: Do you support the natural gas reserves tax on the November 7 ballot? If it passed, how would that affect your negotiations with the producers on a gas pipeline?

A: I am opposed. This initiative is akin to taxing income before it is even earned. The way to get an agreement on building a pipeline is to negotiate, not litigate.

Q: Do you support the Petroleum Profits Tax passed by the Legislature and signed into law by Gov. Murkowski? If no, why not?

A: My preference was a tax on the gross price with a price-progressive index. We need to see how companies apply the tax credits within the law. If the credits are abused and Alaska is shortchanged, changes will be proposed. The intent of the credits is to encourage new exploration and infrastructure development.

—*ANCHORAGE DAILY NEWS*, OCTOBER 22, 2006

Alaska's small business owners are the backbone of our regional economies. Small Alaskan-owned businesses should have just as much say in state policy as the big companies do. Our precious businesses are major employers of Alaskans and keep Alaska's money circulating through our economy. As mayor and CEO of the booming city of Wasilla, my team invited investment and encouraged business growth by eliminating small business inventory taxes, eliminated personal property taxes, reduced real property tax mill levies every year I was in office, reduced fees, and built the infrastructure our businesses needed to grow and prosper.

—PALIN-PARNELL CAMPAIGN BOOKLET: *NEW ENERGY FOR ALASKA*, NOVEMBER 3, 2006

I'm certainly a Washington outsider, and I'm proud of that because I think that that is what we need also . . . Reform that actually happens is tough, and you can't just talk about it and you can't just talk about your years of experience in a system—a bureaucratic system. You have to show examples, and what I have done is have been able to show examples as a mayor cutting taxes every year that I was in office, as a governor now, suspending our fuel tax recently, getting our handle on the state's budget in Alaska, growing the surplus so that we can return that surplus right back to the people of Alaska.

—*HANNITY & COLMES*, SEPTEMBER 17, 2008

ON NATIONAL
SECURITY AND
TERRORISM

Q: This year saw the biggest wartime call-up of Alaska National Guard troops ever. Combined with deployments of active-duty forces, thousands of Alaskans are now serving in Iraq, Afghanistan and elsewhere overseas. What's your view of the Iraq war, and do you support Pres. Bush's "war on terror"?

A: I support President Bush's efforts to stop terrorism by taking the fight to the terrorists. In the Iraq war, I would like to see the president develop an exit strategy to get our troops home.

—*Anchorage Daily News*, October 22, 2006

I think it was quite unfortunate that, to me, it was a fear of being politically incorrect to not—I'm going to use the word—profile this guy [Fort Hood shooter Nidal Hasan]. Profiling in the sense of finding out what his radical beliefs were; simple things like looking at his business card that had the secret codeword [an apparent reference to the initials SOA (Soldier of Allah) that Nidal printed on his cards]. Now, because I used the word profile, I'm going to get clobbered tomorrow morning. The liberals, their heads are just going to be spinning. They're going to say she is radical, she is extreme. But I say profiling in the context of doing whatever we can to save innocent American lives; I'm all for it then.

—COMMENTING ON THE FACT THAT WARNING SIGNS OF NIDAL HASAN'S RADICALISM WERE MISSED DUE TO POLITICAL CORRECTNESS, *IRAN TIMES INTERNATIONAL*, WASHINGTON DC, NOVEMBER 27, 2009

I'm comfortable with Barack Obama as our commander-in-chief assuming that he has those around him who recognize, as I'm sure he will recognize also, if he doesn't already, that terrorists have not changed their mind. They still would seek to destroy America and our allies, and all that it is that we hold dear to us. Democratic values and our freedoms . . . I am sure that Barack Obama will surround himself with those who recognize what the threat is, and will know how to deal with the threat.

—*THE TODAY SHOW*, NOVEMBER 11, 2008

*My position has always been that we need oil, and if we
don't drill for it here where we have the strictest standards
and environmental concerns than anywhere else in the
world, we're going to have to drill for oil elsewhere, where
they don't have those standards, and we're going to have to be
more reliant on foreign regimes who don't like America.*

—AFTER THE BP OIL SPILL, *ON THE RECORD WITH GRETA VAN SUSTEREN*, MAY 14, 2010

Q: Your views on national security issues?

A: I think candidates are going to be asked, "Are you doing—and are your intentions to do—all that you can to help secure these United States?" And I think every elected official needs to ask themselves that. And I say that, even personally. My one and only son, my 18-year-old, has just signed up for the United States Army. He is at boot camp right now, and I'm thinking, "You know, this kid is doing all that he can within his power to help secure and defend the United States." Every elected official had better be asking themselves, "Are you doing as much also? Are you doing all that you can?"

—INTERVIEW WITH CHARLIE ROSE, PBS, OCTOBER 12, 2007

If anybody still wants to talk about it, I will. Because this is an unrepentant domestic terrorist who had campaigned to blow up, to destroy our Pentagon and our U.S. Capitol.

—ON BARACK OBAMA'S TIES TO FORMER WEATHER UNDERGROUND MEMBER WILLIAM AYERS, UPI NEWSTRACK, NOVEMBER 12, 2008

Q: We talk on the anniversary of 9/11. Why do you think those hijackers attacked? Why did they want to hurt us?

A: You know, there is a very small percentage of Islamic believers who are extreme, and they are violent, and they do not believe in American ideals, and they attacked us, and now we are at a point here seven years later, on the anniversary, in this post-9/11 world, where we're able to commit to "never again." They see that the only option for them is to become a suicide bomber, to get caught up in this evil, in this terror. They need to be provided the hope that all Americans have instilled in us, because we're a democratic, we are a free, and we are a free-thinking society.

—*E!* INTERVIEW WITH CHARLIE GIBSON, SEPTEMBER 11, 2008

I believe that America has to exercise all options in order to stop the terrorists who are hell-bent on destroying America and our allies. We have got to have all options out there on the table.

—*WASHINGTON POST*, SEPTEMBER 12, 2008

———————

Energy is inherently linked to security and prosperity. More and more Americans are recognizing this also. You can see the constituents putting pressure on Congress to say, "Come on, Congress, get rid of that gridlock that you are so engaged in now." We sort of have a "do-nothing Senate" right now where nobody's wanting to really pick up the ball and run with it and take the steps that we have to take to become more energy independent. And it's going to take a whole change in leadership in order to really crush that gridlock and get going on this.

—*HANNITY & COLMES*, SEPTEMBER 17, 2008

———————

ON THE TEA PARTY MOVEMENT

*This is the future of our country. The tea party
movement is the future of politics.*

—FoxNews.com, February 7, 2010

---

*The great thing about what's going on right now across the
country is that there isn't the apathy that perhaps we had seen
even a year ago. All these people who are getting riled up. It's
a healthy riled up, too. This is good for democracy. It's people
getting sick and tired of feeling disenfranchised and disenchanted
with their government, and they want their voice heard.*

—USA Today, December 11, 2009

I see the danger of more of the same of the mainstream media wanting to paint Tea Partiers as radical, wacko conspiracy theorists.

—On the Tea Party proponents embracing the claims of "birthers" who believe that Barack Obama was not born in the United States, *The Hill*, February 17, 2010

When the GOP strays from the planks in the platform, a people's movement like the Tea Party movement is invited in to kind of hold these politicians accountable again and remind them of their constitutional limits there on the federal level, and it's a beautiful movement. I'm proud to get to be a part of it in terms of at least hearing from those in the Tea Party movement and sharing with them what I believe are some common-sense solutions to the challenges facing us.

—Fox News interview with Chris Wallace, February 7, 2010

Some of you are registered Republicans. Some of you are what we used to call Reagan Democrats. And some of you are like so many of my friends and my family, including my own husband, are just independent, not registered in any party.

—*Natchez* (Mississippi) *Democrat*, March 28, 2010

*We don't like the way the liberal establishment is running
things. We are proud to call ourselves Tea Party Americans.*

—*Detroit News*, May 1, 2010

---

*Because the Tea Party movement is quite reflective of
what the GOP—the planks in the platform—are supposed
to be about limited government and more freedom, more
respect for equality. That's what the Tea Party movement
is about. So I think that the two are much entwined.*

—*Washington Times*, February 8, 2010

---

*This is about the people . . . and it's a lot bigger than
any charismatic guy with a teleprompter.*

—*Reuters*, February 7, 2010

---

*Some reporters are trying to portray us Tea Party people as racists
or violent or rednecks. I don't mind the redneck part, actually.
But the rest of that is ridiculous—absolutely ridiculous.*

—*Charlotte Observer*, May 14, 2010

Now the smart thing will be for independents who are such a part of this Tea Party movement to, I guess, kind of start picking a party. Which party reflects how that smaller, smarter government steps to be taken? Which party will best fit you? And then because the Tea Party movement is not a party, and we have a two-party system, they're going to have to pick a party and run with one or the other: "R" or "D."

—CBSNews.com, February 17, 2010

ON TINA FEY

I watched [Saturday Night Live] with the volume all the way down. I thought it was hilarious. I thought she was spot-on. . . . They've been saying that for years up in Alaska [that we look alike]. In fact, I dressed up as Tina Fey once for Halloween. We've been doing that before Tina Fey was doing that.

—Commenting on Tina Fey's portrayal of Palin in Saturday Night Live skits, Hannity & Colmes, September 17, 2008

I'd been a fan of SNL for decades, and I have a lot of respect for the present talent. I knew it would be a good thing to be a part of. And also, of course, to let Americans know that I can laugh at myself, too.

—On appearing on Saturday Night Live, Esquire, March 2009

Q: What did you think of Tina Fey, really?

A: I really liked her. Her in-laws came to one of our rallies and met us backstage. They're pretty hardcore Republicans, the in-laws were. She had told me that, she was like, "[B]elieve it or not, I'm from a family of Republicans." You, know, it was like, we have more in common than you think.

—*Anchorage Daily News*, November 9, 2008

I've been really busy. I picked up a gig in Las Vegas at the Legends show, playing Tina Fey.

—*The Tonight Show*, March 2, 2010

ON WASHINGTON

We're headed to being a country that instead of the people deciding how much money our government has, the government is deciding how much money the people can have. And that's backwards . . . It is time to remind them [Washington] that government should be working for us; we should not have to work for the government.

—WorldNetDaily.com, May 14, 2010

So on March 2 you have a clear choice. I want to hear Texas, what's it gonna be: The way they operate in D.C. or the way Y'ALL get things done in Texas?

—Houston Chronicle, February 8, 2010

We believe in the forward movement of freedom,
not the constant expansion of government.

—COLLEGIAN, UNIVERSITY OF RICHMOND, OCTOBER 13, 2008

GRETA VAN SUSTEREN: Congress doesn't have a budget yet. Any thought about that?

SARAH PALIN: You know, even as a city manager and mayor in the city of Wasilla, you have a budget. You work on the budget all year long. You propose it to your lawmakers and the council members who hold the purse strings and you work together on adopting that. I can't believe that a lot of Americans aren't even aware that we don't have a budget! And it amazes me that here again, some in the White House and the administration and Congress, think that's OK, that that's acceptable, since it's not.

—ON THE RECORD WITH GRETA VAN SUSTEREN, MAY 14, 2010

Americans get it. In Washington, they don't get it.

—ORLANDO SENTINEL, MARCH 12, 2010

We don't think the government should take more; we think bureaucracy should do more with less so that you can you can prosper and thrive. You should not be working for government. Your government should be working for you.

—SOUTHEAST MISSOURIAN, OCTOBER 30, 2008

There's no accountability [in government]. And that's why people want to fire those people and bring in new people with a greater sense of what the free-market principles should be.

—THE HILL, MAY 20, 2010

WHAT OTHERS SAY ABOUT SARAH PALIN

We've been campaigning together, and the electricity has been incredible. I'd like to say it's all because of a charisma injection on the part of John McCain, but it's not. They're excited about this reformer, this lifetime member of the NRA, the person who's a point guard. She has it.

—JOHN McCAIN ON HIS RUNNING MATE, SARAH PALIN, *LAS VEGAS REVIEW-JOURNAL*, SEPTEMBER 8, 2008

"Mr. Palin, what does Senator McCain need to know about working with your wife?"

"She's a hard worker, and she's not wired normal."

—*People*, August 29, 2008

The last great speech I heard was delivered by my father. There seems to be a new Reagan—and she's a she.

—The late president Ronald Reagan's son Michael,
Daily Mail (U.K.), September 4, 2008

We have a state that needs new management. [Palin & Parnell] represent a new generation. And they represent a new vision, new energy. They represent the kind of people that ought to come along and take our places. And it needs a new agenda for all of us to get behind. Think of this when you go to vote; don't go to vote alone, and you'll help Sarah become the next governor of Alaska, which we all want to see.

—Alaska senator Ted Stevens on a 2006
Alaska governor ad, October 30, 2006

PEOPLE MAGAZINE: Senator McCain, of all the candidates you considered, what drew you to her?

JOHN MCCAIN: Obviously, I found her to be very intelligent and very well-versed on the issues. But I think the important thing was that she's a reformer. She's taken on special interests since she ran for the PTA and the city council and mayor. The courage, I guess, is what most impressed me.

—*People*, August 29, 2008

We definitely want a governor [as McCain's vice-presidential nominee], but slim pickings, though, in the governors . . . Sarah Palin: I like her. She's a beautiful woman, but she's also a conservative. Her husband, he's a fisherman. I'm not kidding you, and they go out and fish on the weekends. He's a commercial fisherman. I'm telling you, I think that sells. That sells a lot more than "my friends" and comprehensive immigration reform. And she's not for comprehensive reform, I can tell you that right now. She's sick to death of this immigration nonsense in the United States.

—Laura Ingraham on her radio show, March 10, 2008

One of her strengths is being able to hold her tongue when she's been unfairly attacked. By staying true to her beliefs, things always seem to fall into place for her.

—SARAH'S BROTHER CHUCK JR., QUOTED IN *SARAH: HOW A HOCKEY MOM TURNED ALASKA'S POLITICAL ESTABLISHMENT UPSIDE DOWN* BY KAYLENE JOHNSON

She truly listened to what we wanted in our town, and she got it done.

—RICHARD CLAYTON, OWNER OF THE LOCAL BIKE SHOP WHO FOR 20 YEARS HAS BEEN EQUIPPING THE PALINS WITH EVERYTHING FROM SINGLE SPEEDS FOR TRACK TO HANDLEBAR STREAMERS FOR PIPER, ASSOCIATED PRESS, SEPTEMBER 6, 2008

I kind of worried about how she would do up there on stage. You have to have a certain go-get-'em to get up there and stand up for yourself, and she came across as such a shy, sweet girl.

—HAIRDRESSER DIANE OSBORNE, WHO HELPED YOUNG WOMEN GET READY FOR BEAUTY PAGEANTS. IN 1984 SHE MET THEN SARAH HEATH, AGE 20, *NEW YORK TIMES*, OCTOBER 23, 2008

Governor Palin is very charismatic and personable. If you meet her on the street, she will greet you by name, mention your children's names, and ask a relevant question about your family. She's organized, a multitasker; she's a "super woman" who has it all. She has tapped into an anti-intellectual strain in America. Her greatest strength is her confidence—the "not blinking" rhetoric. However, not blinking leaves her vulnerable. She doesn't even know what she doesn't know, and she's not open to anyone who wants to tell her what she doesn't know . . . I attended multiple city council meetings when Sarah Palin was mayor of Wasilla, and Sarah had a very informal style. The meetings were not run professionally. Sarah tended to be very lax with Robert's Rules of Order, for instance. In addition, many government meetings were kicked off with a prayer.

—ANNE KILKENNY, RESIDENT OF WASILLA,
ALASKA, SEPTEMBER 21, 2008

Not only does she talk pro-life, she lives pro-life.

—RICHARD LAND, PRESIDENT OF THE SOUTHERN BAPTIST
CONVENTION'S ETHICS AND RELIGIOUS LIBERTIES COMMISSION,
WALL STREET JOURNAL WASHINGTON WIRE, AUGUST 29, 2008

Sarah always did and still does surround herself with people she gets along well with. They protect her, and that's what she needs. She has surrounded herself with people who would not allow others to disagree with Sarah. Either you were in favor of everything Sarah was doing or you had a black mark by your name.

—DARLENE LANGILL, WHO SERVED ON THE WASILLA CITY COUNCIL DURING THE FIRST YEAR OF THE PALIN ADMINISTRATION, *TORONTO STAR*, SEPTEMBER 13, 2008

Frankly, I can't imagine that question being asked of a man. I think it's offensive, and I think a lot of women will find it offensive.

—TALKING WITH REPORTERS, MCCAIN CAMPAIGN STRATEGIST STEVE SCHMIDT TOOK OFFENSE AT THE IDEA THAT PALIN MIGHT HAVE TROUBLE JUGGLING THE VICE PRESIDENCY AND HER FAMILY OBLIGATIONS, *LOS ANGELES TIMES*, SEPTEMBER 4, 2008

I'm not sure what she brings to the ticket other than she's a woman and a conservative. Well, she's a better speaker than McCain. People will say she hasn't been on the national scene long enough. But I believe she's a quick study.

—MOTHER-IN-LAW, FAYE PALIN, QUOTED IN THE *NEW YORK DAILY NEWS*, AUGUST 31, 2008

It's something I think most Alaskans won't approve of. It's not something we love. We love the musher who drives on through the storm to the finish, not the musher who quits halfway.

—Alaska senator Hollis French on Palin
quitting the governorship, quoted by
KTUU-TV (Anchorage), July 3, 2009

It's incredibly hypocritical that Sarah Palin, who disapproves of government involvement in just about anything, now suddenly wants the government to help people be religious. It is wildly inconsistent with her views on limited government to get the government involved in matters of faith.

—Barry Lynn, the executive director of Americans
United for Separation of Church and State,
quoted by ABCnews.com, April 20, 2010

I remember asking Sarah why she would enter a beauty pageant when that seemed so prissy to the rest of us. She told me matter of factly, "It's going to help pay my way through college."

—Sarah's brother Chuck Jr., quoted in Sarah:
How a Hockey Mom Turned Alaska's Political
Establishment Upside Down by Kaylene Johnson

I don't think Sarah ever wanted to lead. She wanted to be a good girl and play by the rules, but she wasn't someone who was trying to break new ground or argue about things or voice an opinion. In a way she was almost a wallflower type. I'm not sure what happened between then and now, but something must have.

—COLLEGE FRIEND LORI ANN PERRIN,
NEW YORK TIMES, OCTOBER 23, 2008

I think what I heard from the governor really had to do with the weight on her, the concern she had for the cost of all the ethics investigations and the like—the way that that weighed on her with respect to her inability to just move forward Alaska's agenda on behalf of Alaskans in the current context of the environment. So that's what I saw.

—SEAN PARNELL, LIEUTENANT GOVERNOR OF
ALASKA, WHO SUCCEEDED SARAH PALIN WHEN SHE
RESIGNED, *NEW YORK TIMES*, JULY 5, 2009

Governor Palin has captivated everyone on both sides of the political spectrum and we are excited to add her dynamic voice to the FOX News lineup.

—FOX HAS SIGNED A MULTIYEAR DEAL WITH SARAH PALIN FOR HER TO OFFER POLITICAL COMMENTARY AND ANALYSIS ON THE CABLE CHANNEL, AS WELL AS FOX'S WEB SITE, RADIO NETWORK, AND BUSINESS CABLE CHANNEL. SHE ALSO WILL HOST OCCASIONAL EPISODES OF FOX NEWS' *REAL AMERICAN STORIES*, A SERIES THAT WILL FEATURE INSPIRATIONAL STORIES ABOUT AMERICANS, BILL SHINE, EXECUTIVE VICE PRESIDENT OF PROGRAMMING, AMERICA'S INTELLIGENCE WIRE, JANUARY 12, 2010

PEOPLE MAGAZINE: Mr. Palin, you have this tiny baby with special needs. Do you worry that people may wonder if she'll be giving short shrift to her family?

TODD PALIN: She's heard that her whole life—the challenges of being a female and mother in the work force. I remember the first time she ran for mayor one of her fellow council members told her you can't run because you've got three negatives: Track, Bristol and Willow. Those are the three kids we had at the time. So when you tell her that kind of stuff, she just gets fired up. We're an Alaska family that adapts.

—*PEOPLE*, AUGUST 29, 2008

Sarah Palin's desire to settle old scores, while doing little to add to her credibility, does generously add to the ongoing soap opera that is the Republican Party. We wish her the best of luck on her [book] tour.

—Democratic National Committee spokesman
Hari Sevugan, *The Hill*, November 17, 2009

We should all be proud of Governor Sarah Palin's historic nomination, and I congratulate her and Senator McCain. While their policies would take America in the wrong direction, Governor Palin will add an important new voice to the debate.

—Senator Hillary Clinton, in a written statement
congratulating Sarah Palin on being named vice
presidential candidate, ABC news, August 29, 2008

Part of it is she's so much one of us. As absolutely drop dead gorgeous as this woman is on the outside, I'm here to testify she's 20 times more beautiful on the inside.

—Minnesota Representative Michele
Bachmann, *Minnesota Daily*, April 7, 2010

I am honored and grateful to have Sarah Palin's support. She, too, is a political outsider and a strong fiscal conservative, and we share a common concern for the direction our country is headed in under Barbara Boxer and her allies in Washington.

—Carly Fiorina, the ex–Hewlett Packard CEO, on Sarah Palin's support for the Republican U.S. Senate nomination from California, *Eweek.com*, May 7, 2010

Now we know why liberal Democrats hate and fear Sarah Palin. Sarah Palin is the next Ronald Reagan. In less than a week, Governor Sarah has captured the heart and soul of this convention, the Republican Party, and the conservative movement. She brings together social conservatives, and economic conservatives and libertarians, and people who are fed up with the Culture of Corruption that infests our nation's politics. From this moment forward, there's no limit on where Sarah Palin might go.

—Richard A. Viguerie, chairman of ConservativeHQ.com, quoted by US Newswire, September 4, 2008

It is a tremendous honor to receive Governor Palin's endorsement. Sarah Palin has energized the conservative movement like few others in our generation.

—NIKKI HALEY, WHILE SHE WAS RUNNING FOR
GOVERNOR OF SOUTH CAROLINA IN A PRIMARY
ELECTION, UPI NEWSTRACK, MAY 14, 2010

First of all, she's got an incredible future in right-wing politics. She could do anything that she wanted from talk radio show. She could be governor. Obviously, she filibustered pretty good tonight. She could go into the Senate. Her main problem is that people don't view her as substantive enough, as Ari pointed out, in a lot of areas to be a candidate for national office. I don't think she advanced that ball any with the interview tonight. She's got four years in—three years before it all starts again. So she's got time to deal with that. I don't think she helped herself in that sense. Maybe there were some things, she had some things on her mind that she wanted to talk about. Obviously she got to do that. Who can fault her for doing that?

—DEMOCRATIC STRATEGIST JAMES CARVILLE ON
LARRY KING LIVE, NOVEMBER 12, 2008

JOHN MCCAIN: I'm very grateful that she agreed to run with me. She inspired people. She still does. And look, I couldn't be happier with Sarah Palin. And she's going back to be a great governor, and I think she will play a big role in the future of this country.

JAY LENO: Did she ever get off message at one point?

MCCAIN: Did you expect mavericks to stay on message? We did a lot of things together, a lot of these rallies. The people were very excited and inspired by her. And that's what really mattered, I think. Look, she's a great reformer. She took on the governor of her own party when she ran for governor.

LENO: Gotcha.

MCCAIN: She understands all the energy issues. There's a $40 billion pipeline coming to bring natural gas to places like California. And so look, she's a marvelous person.

—*TONIGHT SHOW*, NOVEMBER 11, 2008

She is currently the single most powerful political person in the country. The day she announces for president, she gives that up.

—SUPPORTER OF SARAH PALIN, SID DINERSTEIN,
GOP CHAIRMAN IN FLORIDA'S PALM BEACH
COUNTY, ASSOCIATED PRESS, JULY 2, 2010

Because she's enthusiastic and positive, she can be misread as naive and someone who can be manipulated. I think [Alaska Republican Committee Chief] Randy Ruedrich and [Governor Frank Murkowski's chief of staff] Jim Clark misread her . . . I think that people who wanted her to look the other way assumed that she would play ball.

—TUCKERMAN BABCOCK, A FORMER REPUBLICAN PARTY
CHAIRMAN AND LONGTIME PALIN ADVISER, *KNIGHT-
RIDDER/TRIBUNE BUSINESS NEWS*, OCTOBER 24, 2006

Much of Wasilla has given way to strip malls and subdivisions. Palin knows this is the heart of her town. In 1999, when Wal-Mart was the place to shop in Wasilla, a couple who worked there decided to get married in the aisles of the store. Shoppers convened, and tour-bus passengers stopped and gawked. Palin, who was then mayor of the 5,000 or so residents of the town, officiated. Later, she told a reporter that she had to hold back tears. "It was so sweet," she said. "It was so Wasilla."

—AMANDA COYNE IN *NEWSWEEK*, SEPTEMBER 22, 2008

Dreams are important. Ronald Reagan once said everyone has a heroic right to dream great dreams. Governor Sarah Palin took that set of musings in my mind and the words that had been wonderful sentiments from President Reagan and turned it into a genuine reality in my life for an opportunity I could not have dreamed of.

—PALMER ALASKA ATTORNEY TALIS COLBERG, AFTER BEING NAMED ALASKA ATTORNEY GENERAL BY GOVERNOR SARAH PALIN, *KNIGHT-RIDDER/TRIBUNE BUSINESS NEWS*, DECEMBER 14, 2006

ABOUT THE EDITOR

Matt Lewis is a writer, blogger, and commentator based in Alexandria, Virginia. He currently serves as a Senior Contributor for the *Daily Caller*. A former columnist for *Politics Daily*, Lewis hosts *The Matt Lewis Show* podcast, and cohosts *The Week in Blog*, a weekly diavlog on Bloggingheads.TV.

Previously, he served as a contributing writer and blogger for Townhall.com. Matt has appeared on Fox News, MSNBC, CNN, and C-SPAN, as well as on numerous radio shows, including *The G. Gordon Liddy Show*, *Lou Dobbs*, and NPR's *Talk of the Nation*. He has been quoted by major publications, such as the *Washington Post* and the *New York Times*, and has authored columns and blogs for diverse publications, including *Politico*, *Human Events Online*, the *Daily Caller*, *Big Government*, and *Campaigns & Elections Magazine*.

www.mattlewis.org
Quotable Rogue on Twitter: @QuotableRogue
Quotable Rogue hashtag: #PalinQuotes

INDEX

Iron Dog snow machine race, 13
Israel, 90, 92
Jewish settlements in Israel, 90
Juneteenth Day, 41
Kagan, Elena, 108
Kempthorne, Dirk, 73
Kilkenny, Richard, 170
lame ducks
    governors as, 27
    Reagan as, 28
Land, Richard, 170
Langill, Darlene, 171
leadership by America, 16
Ledbetter pay act, 39
Letterman, David, 81, 82
Lewis, C.S., 122
liberal establishment, 159
    Democrats' view of Palin, 176
libraries, banned books, 40
Lieberman, Joe, x
Limbaugh, Rush, 23
lipstick, 32
LNG (Liquid Natural Gas) project, 62
love of country, 35
Lynn, Barry, 172
marijuana, 50, 51
marriage
    advice to Bristol, 84
    defining, 38, 39
mayor, Palin as, 139
McCain, John, ix, xi, 103–106, 121
    and Obama's energy plan, 69
    on Palin as vp candidate, 168
    on S. Palin, 166, 178
media, 107–114
    relationships with, 147
Michigan, campaign closing in, 33
military, son in, 83, 85, 98, 154
misinformation, 111
Moe, Tom, 105
Monegan, Walt, firing of, 25
moose stew, 9